About the Author

Lawrence Harte is the president of Althos, an expert information provider covering the communications industry. He has over 29 years of technology analysis, development, implementation, and business management experience. He has setup, managed, and provided training for keyword advertising, search engine optimization, affiliate links, and email broadcast marketing programs. Mr. Harte has interviewed hundreds of Internet marketing experts and tested many types of web marketing systems to discover the key success principles used for Internet marketing programs. Mr. Harte's combined knowledge and experience in business systems, communications technologies allow him to communicate well with all people within a company that have a need to understand marketing programs and communication systems. He has authored over 100 books on communications technologies and systems on topics including Internet Marketing, Business Finance, Mobile Communications, IP Telephony, and Billing Systems. Mr. Harte holds many degrees and certificates include an Executive MBA from Wake Forest University (1995) and a BSET from the University of the State of New York, (1990).

Introduction to Internet Marketing

Lawrence Harte

ALTHOS
SIMPLIFYING KNOWLEDGE

Althos Publishing
Fuquay-Varina, NC 27526 USA
Telephone: 1-800-227-9681
Fax: 1-919-557-2261
email: info@althos.com
web: www.Althos.com

Althos

Copyright © 2008 By Althos Publishing
First Printing

Printed and Bound by Lightning Source, TN.

Every effort has been made to make this manual as complete and as accurate as possible. However, there may be mistakes both typographical and in content. Therefore, this text should be used only as a general guide and not as the ultimate source of information. Furthermore, this manual contains information on telecommunications accurate only up to the printing date. The purpose of this manual to educate. The authors and Althos Publishing shall have neither liability nor responsibility to any person or entity with respect to any loss or damage caused, or alleged to be caused, directly or indirectly by the information contained in this book.

International Standard Book Number: 1-932813-25-X

Table of Contents

Internet Marketing

Internet marketing is the process of communicating marketing and sales information using the Internet. To be successful at Internet marketing, it doesn't matter if you are an expert in marketing or a novice. However, it does matter that you can identify, setup, and test different marketing campaigns and programs.

Some of the advantages of using Internet marketing programs include rapid response, the ability to precisely measure customer interactions with promotions, the ability to control of how and where money is spent, the ability to precisely target who sees promotional materials and cost effective marketing programs.

Internet Marketing Advantages

Internet marketing advantages include getting rapid response from marketing campaigns, tracking interaction with promotional materials, flexible spending controls, precise targeting and cost effective marketing programs.

Rapid Response

Internet marketing programs often can have measurable results within days or hours compared to other forms of media such as radio broadcast, direct mail or media publications. The ability to measure rapid response also allows for the content or promotion to be changed or adapted in mid-promotion increasing the overall effectiveness of the program.

Tracking Interaction

Unlike traditional marketing, Internet marketing offers the possibility to track almost every action a visitor or potential customer takes in response to marketing messages and how they navigate through their buying cycle. Tracking codes can be inserted into links and stored in cookies to find out how web site visitors and email customers react to your marketing programs.

Spending Control

Internet marketing programs commonly have threshold settings allowing limits to be established for campaigns. The program is run until the budget threshold is reached and the promotion slots are give to other promoters. This allows merchants to budget and test multiple campaigns where other forms of media such as magazines require a single promotion that reaches many people. Some Internet marketing programs also have pay for performance programs such as affiliate marketing where the cost of promotion only occurs when sales or qualified sales leads have occurred.

Precise Targeting

Internet marketing programs can use precise targeting by placing ads only in front of potential customers that have a very defined set of characteristics. This means that the ads can be adjusted for those types of customers (microtargeting), making the ads more effective. For example, an airline can promote special airfare rates between cities where airline customers have repeatedly traveled. The ad can be customized to show the cities where the special rates apply which closely match the interests of the potential customer.

Cost Effective Marketing

Internet marketing can be cost effective (not always). The cost to communicate with potential customers through the Internet is low, which allows the promoter to cost effectively reach customers in large geographic areas. Internet marketing can have a higher cost per transaction (such as advertising on search engines) with a lower overall promotional cost. This is because the advertiser may pay for the transaction cost rather than the presentation, which can result in lower overall marketing costs.

While some Internet marketing programs can be complex, almost anyone can utilize certain types of Internet marketing. With a bit of planning, organization and testing, self-managed Internet marketing programs can be very effective. Some marketing agencies now specialize in Internet marketing programs while other marketing agencies do not yet understand the differences between traditional marketing and Internet marketing.

Changes in Internet Marketing

Since many of the Internet marketing programs and metrics were introduced in the 1990s, they are still relatively new and continuously changing. Marketing techniques that may have worked well in the late 1990s may have decreased in effectiveness or even be not usable now.

Promotion Saturation

Promotion saturation is the over promotion of a product or service. When consumers are overwhelmed by media promotions, they become desensitized and ignore or bypass advertising promotions. This results in much lower response rates. An example of promotion saturation is the overuse of banner ads. As a result, the click through rate for banner ads has decreased to below

½%.

Customer Ad Filtering

In response to over promotion, customers are setting up ad filters (such as SPAM filters) to remove unwanted promotion messages. This means that it is getting much harder to reach prospective customers even when the ad is actually sent to their address.

Shift to Pull Marketing

Marketing programs are shifting from one-way broadcast promotions (TV, radio, and magazines) to interactive advertising (Internet portal ads and search marketing). The revenue streams for pull marketing programs are increasing by more than 70% compared to stagnant or decreasing marketing dollars spent on traditional broadcast media.

Increasing Internet Marketing Costs

An example of increasing Internet marketing costs is the pay per click cost trend in adword marketing programs. When they were introduced in the early 2000s, the cost per click was low (about 5-10 cents per click) and the response rates (2% to 5%) were high. As adword marketing programs evolved, the cost per click has increased (now over 50 cents per click) along with the cost of fraud while the response rates (about 1/2% to 1%) have decreased.

Internet Marketing Options

There are various types of Internet marketing programs that have a unique mix of advantages and challenges along with economic factors.

Web portals are web pages that have a specific function or focus area. Search engine optimization (SEO) is the process or processes that adjust web site software and content to improve the relative ranking of the search engine list results from keyword searches. Affiliate marketing is the process of sharing marketing and sales programs, compensating marketing affiliates (partners) for their role in communicating and selling to their customers.

Adword marketing is a process that uses keywords that potential customers search for in search engines to display ads. Email marketing is the sending of marketing and sales information using email messaging systems. Affiliate marketing is the process of working with other companies to cross-promote products or services in return for an incentive (affiliate commission).

Banner advertising is the insertion of graphic images on web sites that contain hyperlinks to other web sites. Mobile advertising programs can reach specific types of users in controlled geographic locations. Blogging and Podcast marketing programs can cost effectively reach users that share well defined interests and needs with each other. Viral marketing is the process of promoting and selling products or services through the use of messages or ads that are self regenerative (passed along by recipients).

To increase the effectiveness of Internet marketing, different types of marketing programs can be combined to interact with each other (integrated marketing). A good understanding of the operation, options and economics of the different types of Internet marketing programs can help to determine how to optimize each of the Internet marketing programs and discover how to increase their effectiveness when they are used together.

Figure 1.1 shows some Internet marketing program types. Internet market-

Marketing Program	Description
Search Engine Optimization (SEO)	Getting listed and improving the ranking in search engine results.
Public Relations (PR)	Getting published in other media channels by providing press information.
Banner Advertising	Displaying graphic ads on web sites.
Adword Marketing	Getting ads (typically text ads) on search engines and other web sites that match keywords.
Affiliate Marketing	Promoting products or services through other related companies.
Email Marketing	Sending promotional materials to people via email or messaging services.
Link Exchange	Getting inbound links placed on other web sites as a result of providing reciprocal links on your web site.
Podcasts	Broadcasting media to a list of registered people.
Blogging	Online forums that allow people to ask, discuss, review and answer questions on specific subject areas.

Figure 1.1, Internet Marketing Program Types

ing programs may include search engine optimization, public relations, banner advertising, adword marketing, affiliate marketing, email broadcasting, link exchanges, podcasting and blogging.

Buying Cycle

A buying cycle is the processes and tasks that are used by a person or company when they are buying or replacing a product or service. The steps in a typical Internet buying cycle include discovering a need, researching potential products, gathering comparative information, requesting information and making a purchase decision. The buying cycle for Internet customers tends to be short and can range from days to weeks. An example of buying cycle time is the number of days it takes for a user to buy a car from the time a purchase request is submitted. The cycle is approximately 13 days [1].

During the buying cycle, the potential customer may be influenced by external events that alter their normal buying cycle process. Understanding the buying cycle for specific types of customers can assist in the development and use of Internet marketing campaigns to influence the customers buying decision.

Discovery Phase

The discovery phase of a buying cycle is the point where a person develops an awareness of a need or want. This may occur during an advertising message that identifies how a problem can be solved using a product or service.

Interest Phase

The interest phase of a buying cycle is the reinforcement of the desire for a person to obtain or use a product or service. This may be in the form of repeating the original benefits or showing additional satisfying experiences the user may experience from the product or service.

Research Phase

The research phase of a buying cycle is the period a user spends looking for solutions to obtain the product or service. The goal of a marketing program during the research phase is to get the visitor to bookmark the site or remember the URL for their buying phase.

Buying Phase

The buying phase of a buying cycle is the time the user spends purchasing the product or service. The goal of a marketing program during the buying cycle is to make the purchase transaction as quick and simple as possible for the customer and to avoid triggering doubt in the customer's mind that there is something wrong with the company that is selling the product or service (such as not having contact information on the web page).

Figure 1.2 shows an example of an Internet buying cycle. This example shows a buying cycle for a person who is looking to buy a mobile telephone. This example shows that the prospective customer becomes aware that they have a need or desire for a new mobile telephone after seeing an ad for a new feature. Over time, the consumer's interest for the new phone is developed as the person sees additional ads showing the benefits to using the new feature. When the customer's desire is great enough, a research phase begins

Figure 1.2, Sample Internet Buying Cycle

in which they find out where to buy the product and what options they have to purchase it. When the customer decides to purchase, they will perform a comparison of the vendors who offer the product to determine the best value (prices, shipping time).

Internet Marketing Objectives

Marketing objectives are statements that identify targets that should be achieved through media communication efforts that may include such items as revenue, quantities, market share, account types or experience.

Revenue Targets

Revenue targets are sales values that are desired along with the associated time periods that the sales should be achieved. Revenue targets for marketing programs may be defined in gross sales, net sales, or average revenue sales per customer.

Product Quantities

Product quantity targets are item quantity sales that are desired along with the time period in which they should be sold, shipped or ordered. Product quantity targets for marketing programs may be defined as quantity sold for each marketing campaign or quantity sold per sale (items ordered by each customer).

Product Usage

Marketing campaigns may be used to build awareness of new uses or applications for existing products. An example of a product usage objective is the promotion of how computer printers can be used to print postage labels or t-shirt transfers as a way to encourage consumers to purchase additional materials such as printer ink cartridges.

List Creation

Internet marketing campaigns may be used to gather contact data for potential customers for mailing lists or sales leads. An example of a list creation campaign would be to offer a free product or information document if a person provides their contact information along with some qualifying information (such as interest areas).

Profit Margins

Internet marketing campaigns can be used to promote products or services that have profit margins (such as high-margin items). This may be necessary to ensure that promotional programs are profitable if the cost of Internet marketing has a high marketing cost per sale.

Experience

Marketing campaigns may be performed to gain experience or to discover business metrics such as conversion rates, average sale amount, product return rates and the amount of fraud that is expected to occur.

Domain Names

A domain name is the unique text or sequence of characters that is used to identify an Internet protocol address (IP address) of the web site host computer. Each web site has a unique unchanging IP address. A text domain name is converted into the web site IP address through the use of domain name service (DNS). DNS computers are located throughout the Internet and when they receive a request, they convert the domain text address into the numeric IP address that is used to transfer packets to their destination web site. You can lookup the numeric IP address for a web address by going to www.ip-address.com.

Domain Name Selection

Domain name selection is the process of identifying potential names that people use for connecting to web sites, determining if the domain name is available and registering the domain name. Domains should typically be unique, short, simple to pronounce and easy to remember.

Domain names are composed of a host name and an extension, which can be up to 255 characters long. The extensions are the highest level domain name (such as .com, .org and .net). Extensions have implied meanings for the purpose or type of domain name and some extensions are assigned to a country (such as ".ca" for Canada).

Domains are authorized for use by Internet Corporation for Assigned Names and Numbers (ICANN). Some domain name extensions can be used for virtually any use (.com, .net, .org). Other domain name extensions have some use type requirements before they can be assigned (.gov, .mil, .int). Some country assigned domain names have been used for alternative purposes such as .tv (country of Tuvali) and .co (country of Columbia).

Domain names are commonly composed of text characters but some special characters can be used such as the hyphen (-). When the domain is separated by hyphens, search engines may find and better categorize the domain name.

Figure 1.3 shows some of the domain name types and their common associ-

Extension	Meaning
.com	Commercial
.net	Network
.org	Organization
.edu	Education
.gov	Government
.mil	Military
.int	International Treaty
.info	Information
.biz	Business
.name	Name
.pro	Professional
.mobi	Mobile
.tv	Commonly used for Entertainment Actually means the country of Tuvalu
.co	Commonly used for Company Actually meand Coutnry of Columbia)

Figure 1.3, Domain Name Types

ated uses. The first 7 extensions that were authorized included .com (commercial), .net (network), .org (organization), .edu (education), .gov (government), .mil (military), and .int (international treaty). Additional domain names were authorized including .biz (business), .info (information), .name (name), .pro (professional), and .mobi (mobile). Domain names for certain countries have been used for alternative applications such as .tv (country of Tuvalu) and .co (country of Columbia).

Domain Name Registration

Domain name registration is the process of submitting a domain name registration to a domain registrar. A domain registrar is a company or organization that is authorized by ICANN to issue and manage domain names. A domain holder is a company or person who has the right to use a domain name for a specified period of time (typically in multiples of 1 year).

The first step in the domain name registration process is to check for domain name availability. You can check for availability by visiting a web registrar site (such as www.icdomainnames.com). If the domain name is available, it should be registered with the registrar. To register the domain name, contact information must be provided.

After the domain name is registered, the name must be pointed to the IP address of the web site host site. The host of the web site will provide the unchanging (static) IP address. The domain name registrar (which may also be the web site host) will then broadcast the domain name and its assigned IP address to various packet routers in the Internet. These routers relay this information to other routers in the Internet until eventually all the routers learn the necessary information that will enable them to convert the domain name to the IP address. This process can take several hours or even days.

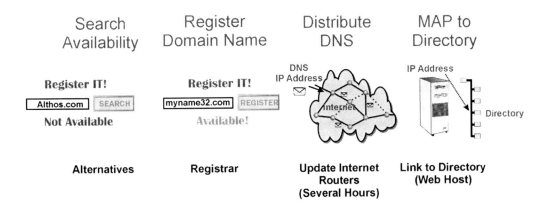

Figure 1.4, Domain Name Registration and Pointing

During the domain name updating process, domain name pointing may work in some geographic areas and not in other areas.

Figure 1.4 shows how the domain name registration process works. The company or person researches and selects a domain name that is not used. The domain name is then submitted to a registrar who creates a registration record, which contains contact information and the address of the server where the domain name will be located.

Once a domain name has been pointed to the web site host computer, the manager of the host computer must assign (map) the domain name to the folder and file. The default file that will be linked to the domain name is index.html.

Email Forwarding

Email forwarding is the process of redirecting emails that are received at one address to another address. The email that is forwarded is called an alias email address. The destination address is where the email is redirected. The use of email forwarding allows the user's email address to be redirected if they change companies.

Email forwarding is a feature of a domain name that must be setup by the company that hosts the web site. Many web hosting systems allow the domain owner to self-manage email aliases and their destination addresses.

An email address is composed of a username part and a domain name part. The username part may have structure requirements such as the types of characters (upper case or lower case) that can be used. The domain name part is never case sensitive.

Some email forwarding systems allow for special processing of alias email addresses. For example, a catch-all email address destination address may be setup to get receive all the emails addressed where the user part cannot be identified (such as "info@domain.com" or "sales@domain.com").

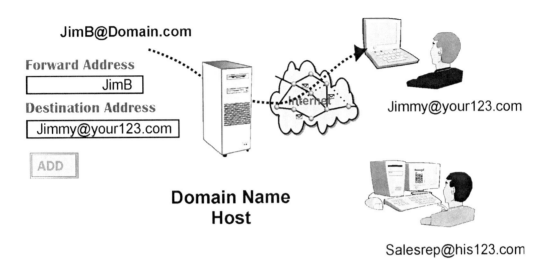

Figure 1.5, Email Forwarding

Figure 1.5 shows how email forwarding may be setup. This domain name has been setup to receive emails and forward them to other email address. The owner of the domain name is provided with an email control panel that allows them to setup alias email addresses and associate them with their destination (forwarding) address. In this example, the email address jimb@domain.com is setup to automatically forward to the email address jimmy@your123.com.

Measuring Internet Marketing Programs

Measuring the success of Internet marketing programs involves tracking the actions web visitors take and converting these actions into values that can be used to determine and compare performance. Some of the common measurements include the number of page hits, page views, ad impressions, click through rates and conversion rates of visitors to web sites.

Page Hits

Page hits are the number of requests to retreive files that is received by web host over a period of time. Because each web page may contain multiple media files (images, audio clips), each request may be counted as a page hit, resulting in a much higher number of hits than web page visitors.

Page Views

Page views are the number of times a web page has been requested and displayed. A page impression is a single access of a web page, which includes all of its referenced media items (pictures, audio files).

Unique Visitors

A unique visitor is web page access by a user that has not visited the web site before. A unique visitor may be identified by their IP address that has not been used before or by unique data (e.g. cookies) that is stored on their computer. The number of unique visitors removes the duplicate count for a visitor who revisits or reloads a web page.

Ad Impressions

Ad impressions are the number of times an advertising message or image has been viewed. Ad impressions indicate how many times an ad is provided to a web browser, not how many times it has been viewed on the display. Ad impressions may not be accurate as a result of various factors that include ads that appear outside the display window (e.g. placed at the end of the web page) or for web pages that load slowly where the user changes web pages before the ad has time to appear.

Click through rate (CTR)

Click through rate is the ratio (usually in percentage form) of how many clicks a link receives from visitors compared to the number of times the link is displayed. An example of click through rate is a link that is clicked 5 times out of 100 displays to visitors is 5%.

Conversion Rates

Conversion rate is a measure of the people who connect to a web page and perform an action (such as purchase a product) via that web site. A high conversion rate percentage usually indicates how much more valuable a web site is to its visitors.

Visitor Tracking

Visitor tracking is the process of assigning a unique identifier (a visitor ID code) to a person who visits a web page that can be used to identify additional pages they visit on the web site. Marketing people want to know where visitors come from (referral site), where they enter, what they look at, how long they stay and where they leave (exit) the web site.

Click Trails

A click trail is the sequence of link selections that specific visitors make between entering and leaving a web site. When a visitor enters into a web site, a connection is made between the visitor's computer and the web site host computer. This creates a new unique session ID and the session ID remains the same while the user is still connected to the web site. This means that any information that the visitor selects when they navigate through the web site (such as items in a shopping cart) can be temporarily stored and associated with the Session ID. When the visitor leaves the web site (or their session ID time period expires), the session ID ends.

Referring URLs

A referring URL is a web link that contains the link destination address along with additional information that identifies the source (the referring URL) or referrer (such as a co-marketing partner) of the visitor.

Figure 1.6 shows some of the ways to measure the effectiveness of Internet marketing programs. This table shows that common Internet marketing measurements range from requests for each object on a single web page to displaying a history of the pages a visitor has accessed after they haveconnected to a web site. Page hits represent the items that are requested by a visitor and can include many objects (such as multiple pictures). Page view displays are the number of complete presentations of a web page for a visi-

Measurement	Description
Page Hits	A request for each item on a web site (There can be many items in a single web page).
Page Views	The number of complete web page presentations.
Pages Viewed per Visitor	How many web pages a visitor goes to during their visit to the web site. A larger number indicates visitors are interested in the web page products or subject area.
Clicks	How many link selections (hyperlink or image links) were performed by visitors.
Unique Clicks	How many non-repeated link selections were made by visitors (removes double and triple clicks by the same visitor).
Conversions	The ratio of actions that resulted from visits or clicks.
Click Trails	The history of web pages visited by each web site visitor.

Figure 1.6, Internet Marketing Measurements

tor. The number of pages viewed per visitor can be an indication on how interested visitors are in the web site content. Clicks are the number of links selected by web page visitors. Unique clicks are the number of links that are selected by different visitors. Conversions are a measure (usually in percentage) of how many actions (such as purchases) resulted from web visits. Click trails are a history of the web pages that each visitor went to during their visit to the web site.

Web Site

A web site is a file or group of files located on a computer (a web host) that is connected to the Internet. These files are generally accessible by other users that are connected to the Internet through the use of a web address. These files may be accessed by a web browser that converts the web site data files into a display format that is viewable by the web site visitor.

Each page on a web site is a data file which may be selected and obtained through the use of Hyperlinks. Hyperlinks are web site and file address tags that can be associated with text, icons or images that, when selected, allow the Hyperlink to redirect the source of information to the address of another document or file. These documents or files may be located anywhere the link address can be connected to.

To transfer files to the web site, you use a file transfer protocol (FTP) software application. FTP is similar to a file manager or Windows explorer program that can transfer files between directories on a computer with added security.

FTP may be available as part of a web browser and can be activated by starting the web address with "ftp://" instead of using "http://". After connecting to a web site using ftp, you will typically need to login with a username and password (right click to start the login process). You simply drag

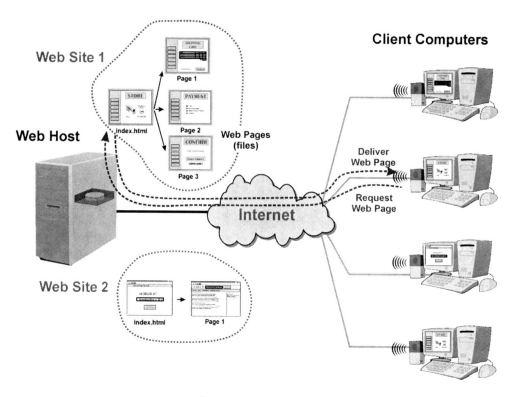

Figure 1.7, Web Site

the files from the source to their destination directories.

Figure 1.7 shows that a web site is a computer (web host) that holds files from multiple web pages for each web site. This example shows that each web page visitor (client computer) requests web pages (files) from the web server (web host). A web site is a group of related web pages and this example shows that a single web host can process many requests for web pages from many users.

Web Page

A web page is a file located on a computer that is connected to the Internet that has a format which allows the file to display (format) information on a user's display (web browser).

Web pages are typically text files that are written in a language that a web browser program can understand (such as hypertext markup language – HTML). Because HTML language is standardized, web pages can be transferred and used regardless of the type of computer system.

A web page begins with a definition of the language that the web page uses (e.g. HTML). This is optionally followed by information that describes the

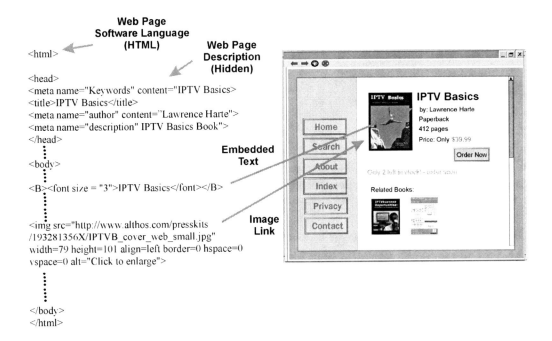

Figure 1.8, Web Page

contents and functions of the web page. Each description type (such as title, or keywords) is contained in a meta-tag. The meta-tag information is hidden from the web browser's display.

The body of the web page contains the content or reference links to content that will be displayed on the user's web browser. The body also contains the formatting information to determine where and how the information is presented in the web browser.

Figure 1.8 shows that a web page is a text file that defines and selects content and coordinates its position on a users display. The web page begins by defining the language it will be using (such as HTML). This is followed (optionally) by meta-tag information that describes the content and purpose of the web page. The body of the web page contains a mix of content such as text and images. Some content may be stored externally to the web page file and referenced (linked). Page formatting information is contained in the body of the web page to determine where and how information is presented on the web page.

Dynamic Web Page

A dynamic web page is a web page file that can have some or all of its information content modified when it is transferred to the user. An example of a dynamic web page is a web page that lists items at an online auction. The auction prices constantly changes so the web page is dynamically created from bid information each time the user requests or refreshes the web page.

Because a dynamic web page is a web page that can have some or all of information content modified when it is transferred to the user, challenges can occur with the listing of the web page in search engines.

Web Page Tables

Web pages can use tables to control the position of text and other media items. A HTML table is a defined display structure that includes lines ("rows") and columns ("cells") that can hold text, images or video media. HTML tables can be placed inside each other (nested) to produce complex presentations of images and data.

The size and structure of tables can be defined in pixels or various other units. How the data in the rows and cells is positioned can also be controlled

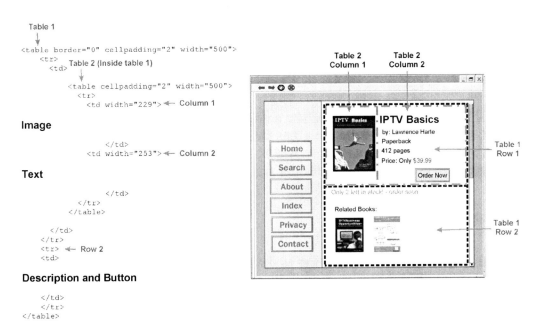

Figure 1.9, HTML Tables

("Left", "Center", or "Right") along with different attributes (color, emphasis). The borders, padding (buffer area) and shading of the tables can also be defined and controlled for all or portions of the table. Empty tables and empty rows and/or cells can be used to precisely control the layout of a web page.

Figure 1.9 shows how web pages can use tables to control the placement of content on web pages. This diagram shows how tables can be inserted inside tables to produce more controlled graphic displays. The first table (table 1) is composed of two rows (<tr>). The second table (table 2) is located inside the first row of table 1. Table 2 has tow columns (<td>).

Web Page Frames

Web page frames are a web browser layout format that divides a browser display window into several display areas (frames). The use of separate frame display areas allows for a more uniform display of web pages within a web site. An example of the use of frames is the use of a toolbar frame for overall site navigation, a title bar frame to hold a company logo and contact information and a main frame to display the selected items.

Not all browsers process frames the same way. The use of web page frames can be a challenge for search engines that should index a frame component instead of indexing the actual web site. In general, it is more common for developers to use tables to create the same effects as frames on a web page.

Web Site Development

Web site development is the set of tasks and processes that are used to create web sites. Web site development typically includes web site definition (requirements), architecture, site design, web page construction and web site testing.

Web Site Definition

Web site definition is the listing of the media objectives and functional requirements for the web page.

Site Architecture

Web site architecture is the identification and location of web pages, media items and processing functions that will be used by the web site.

Site Design

Web site design is the planning of web pages and navigation systems for a web site. Site design might include the use of storyboards that show the proposed flow of web pages, page layout and some functional processes.

Web Construction

Web construction is the creation of the web page's software and the media items that will be used. Web construction may be performed in a web editor that allows for the software instructions to be automatically created from the text and graphics that are positioned in the web editor.

Site Testing

Web site testing is the performing of operational tests to ensure a website is performing the processes it is supposed to and that the delivery of these services perform with acceptable tolerances (such as short web page load time). Web site testing often involves testing web site functionality using different browsers, different versions of browsers, and multiple computers that have different display sizes and media processing functions.

Web Site Templates

A website template is a set of web pages that contain structural components and media elements (such as page banners) that can be modified to produce a web site. Website templates typically include a home page, about us page, contact page and general web page.

Web site templates can be used to rapidly create professional looking web pages in a short period of time. To make the professional looking website operational, the template is downloaded, key fields (text areas) are changed and the new set of web pages is uploaded.

Web site templates typically come with a set of themes and various functions. The themes are the overall style of the web pages including their images and fonts. The web site functions may include newsletters, online storefronts, services offered by the company, or other web site function.

Templates are commonly provided in either HTML or Flash programming. Web site templates that are provided in HTML can be easily edited in web editors (such as Frontpage). Web sites that come in Flash format, which commonly include interesting animations, may require a Flash program editor to make substantial changes. Web site Flash templates may include a simple text file that allows for the changing of basic data using a text editor (such as changing the company name, address and phone numbers).

Web site templates may be available for free, a fixed license or some other form of usage fee. Free web site templates may require some link back function as part of the agreement to use the web template. An example of a company that supplies web site templates is www.boxedart.com.

Web Site Content

Web site content is the information, data or media that is contained within web pages. Content value is the primary reason why visitors go to web pages and search engines may determine the value of content by the amount of content (number of words), structure of the content, and other valuation methods. Some of the sources of content include clip art, original content (copy writing), affiliate content and data feeds.

Web Site Clip Art

Web site clip art is an existing set of media (fonts, graphic images, photographs, audio clips, animation segments, and video clips) that can be used or inserted into web sites. Clip art for web sites may be free, available for a fixed fee, or available on a usage basis. Free content commonly has embedded content or link connection requirements. An example of a company that supplies web site clip art is www.clipartcollection.com.

Copy Writing

Copy writing is the authoring or creation of text (copy) for a specific communication medium (such as a brochure or web page).

Affiliate

Affiliate content is media that is provided from a business partner (such as a marketing partner). These companies may provide product photos, descriptions or content that can be used on their partner sites. Because companies may have multiple marketing partners, the same content from affiliates may be seen on other web sites.

RSS Data Feeds

An RSS feed is a source of data that is in a format (XML) that can be gathered and used by people who link or subscribe to the RSS data feed source. An example of an RSS feed is a continuous supply of news stories and other recent data or information. RSS aggregator software on the web site can receive data RSS feeds, filter, format, and republish the data on the web page. Using RSS data feeds from good sources, web sites can continuously present new and relevant information to their visitors.

Some media publishers such as magazines, news agencies and industry groups provide RSS feeds as a way to distribute information relative to their industry. These feeds are typically indicated by an RSS button on the web

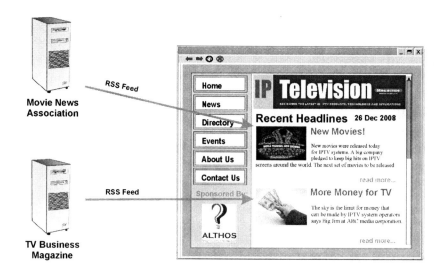

Figure 1.10, RSS Data Feed

site.

RSS feeds can be received and processed using RSS aggregator software. RSS software periodically checks and downloads new RSS items. RSS aggregators can be setup to filter, process, and provide content to a web page.

Figure 1.10 shows how a web site can use multiple RSS data feeds to continuously obtain new content. This example shows that a web site has a dedicated area for RSS data from industry news sources. As news stories that relate to key words for the RSS feed are received, the headlines of the stories are automatically displayed on the news area of the web site.

Metadata

Metadata is information (data) that describes the attributes of other data.

Metadata is contained within meta-tags within the web page software to describe the contents and categorize a web page.

Meta-tags are text identifiers that are used in a web page (such as a HTML or ASP pages) to identify a type of information that will follow. An example of a Meta-tag is <meta name= "description" content= "Web Marketing

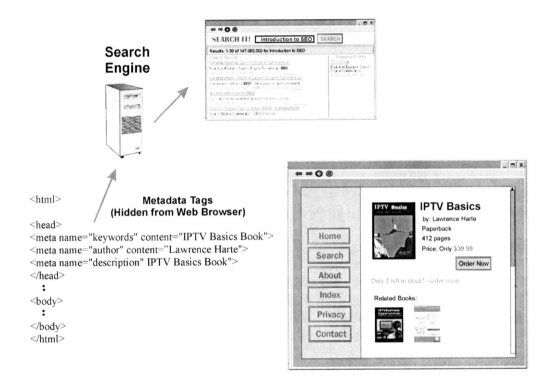

Figure 1.11, Web Page Meta-Tags

Dictionary, Internet Web Marketing Industry Terms and Definitions."

Metadata is divided into categories such as title, keywords, description, author, and other various descriptive categories. Each of these categories can be inserted as separate meta-tags. The browser normally does not display meta-tags.

Figure 1.11 shows how web pages can contain meta-tags (metadata) that help to describe and categorize the web page. This diagram shows a web page containing meta-tags that describe it but are not normally displayed by the web browser. Search engines can use the descriptive metadata to help classify and organize search results.

Web Graphics

Web graphics are diagrams or photos that are formatted in a way that can be used or displayed on web pages. Web graphics are often formatted with a screen resolution of 72 dots per inch (dpi).

When graphics are included in a web page, the web browser must have the capability to read, decode and display it. If the browser cannot display it, the user may be prompted to download a plug-in for the browser that will allow it to display or play the media. To reduce the need for users to download a plug-in media capability for their browser, images are usually stored in common formats such as .bmp, .gif or .jpg formats.

Text may be presented in graphic form instead of using fonts. Graphic text is the presentation of characters that are in image (pixel) format. While graphic text can have any controlled appearance (shape, color and size), graphic text cannot be acquired and processed as normal text. The use of graphic text on web pages may inhibit the ability of search engines to find and index the text content that is presented in graphic form.

When a web graphic is included in a web page, alternative text (alt tag) may be presented to the viewer if the image or other media item cannot be displayed. This alternative text may also be displayed when a user positions the mouse cursor over the image or item that can be displayed or selected.

Web Page Forms

A web page form is a data entry web page that contains a set of information areas (form elements) in which a user can enter data which will be stored or transferred when the user selects the submit button on the form.

The form determines the location of the data entry fields. Data entry fields can be defined as various types including text, passwords, radio buttons, check boxes, lists and other types of data. The form elements (fields) temporarily hold user data until the user selects the "submit" button.

How the user data is processed is determined by the form's action attribute. For example, the action may transfer (post) the data to the end of a file (such as subscribers) or it may send the information to a person via email.

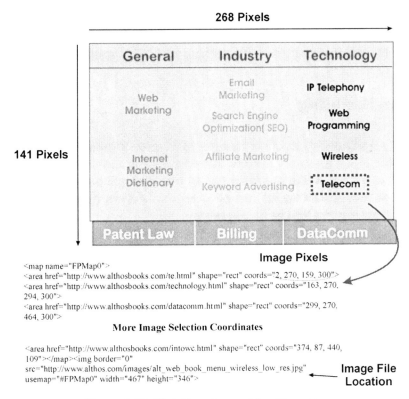

Figure 1.12, Web Page Image Map Operation

Web Page Image Maps

An image map is one or more predefined display areas on a web page that can be selected ("clickable") by a mouse. Image maps are commonly graphic images that are used to help users navigate through a web site.

The image is defined for a screen area. Locations within this graphic area are then defined along with the hyperlink that they will be connected to.

Figure 1.12 shows the basic operation of image maps. This diagram shows that an image map is composed of graphics areas ("hot spots") that the user can select ("clickable") with the mouse. This example shows that the image map is defined for a range (a box) of pixels that are relative to the beginning of the graphic. The HTML code defines the starting and ending location of the image pixels. This is followed by HTML lines that define the image selection coordinates and their associated web link. The information at the end of the HTML instruction defines the name and location of the image file.

Web Page Scripting

The display and operation of web pages can be customized or modified using web page scripts. The use of scripts allows for data that the user has entered to be used to adjust what is presented to the user's web browser. An example of this is how a web script can be used to obtain a new advertising message each time the web page is requested.

Scripts are sets of instructions and data that are processed by the web host computer or the web browser. Web page scripts may use commands from a variety of languages including ASP, Java, Perl, or Microsoft Visual Basic. The script commands may be processed on the web site (server side scripting) or within the user's computer (client side scripting). When the script is performed on the server side, there is more control.

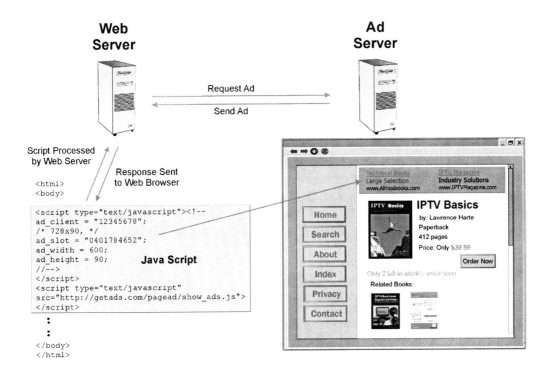

Figure 1.13, Web Page Scripting

Some companies provide sample scripts that can simply be copied and inserted into the web page software. The web server host must be able to understand the script language (e.g. ASP, Java).

Figure 1.13 shows how web page scripting can add additional functions to a web page. This example shows that instructions in a web page initiate a request to an ad server to provide a new ad each time the web page is requested. When the web page is requested, the web server sees the <script> message so it processes those lines of code before providing more information to the web browser. This example shows that the script instructs the web server to obtain a new advertising message and to provide that advertising message to the web browser. After the web server sees the end script (</script>) it continues to process the web page as a regular web page html file.

Cookies

A cookie is a small amount of information that is stored on a web user's computer (a client) that is used by a web site (web server) to help control the content and format of information to the user during future visits to the web site. Cookies may be used to track user visits and store their activity so the system can adapt or customize the presentation to the user during later vis-

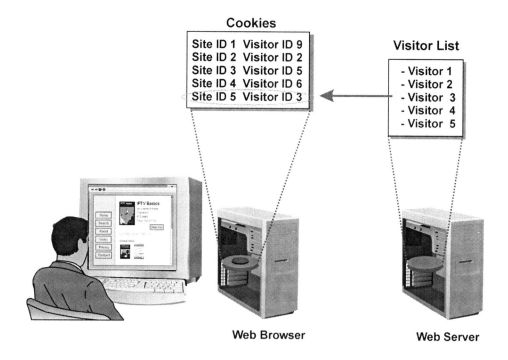

Figure 1.14, Internet Cookies

its.

Cookies are uniquely identified by the web site that stores them and only that web site can retrieve and decode the cookies it stores. Cookies store data in name value pairs. Cookies are only data and cannot command or control programs or other data within the computer where they are stored.

Cookies can store state information such as the shopping cart status (what items are in a shopping cart) or how many times the person has visited a web site. The use of cookies does present some challenges, such as cookies does not work well for people who share the same computer or who have multiple accounts on the same machine.

Figure 1.14 shows the basic operation of Internet cookies. This diagram shows that when a web host receives a connection request from a new visitor, the web host creates a name (visitor ID) and sends a small amount of data that can be stored in a cookies area within the requesting computer. This data is stored as name value pairs and it is only accessible by the host computer (Site ID) that stored the cookie data.

Email Marketing

Email marketing is the process of managing lists, developing ad campaigns, creating promotional offers, broadcasting email messages and tracking the results. Email marketing systems generally combine advanced message broadcast systems along with tracking systems that can monitor the reception, opening, and response to email messages that have been sent.

*** Caution ***

The sending of non-solicited emails has resulted in regulations such as the CAN-SPAM US regulation that was authorized in 2003. The CAN-SPAM act defines the necessary relationship requirements before commercial emails can be sent to recipients to better control the sending of undesired email messages. The penalties for sending unsolicited emails can be severe so checking with a qualified authority (such as an email list management company) can help to avoid or reduce email SPAM penalties.

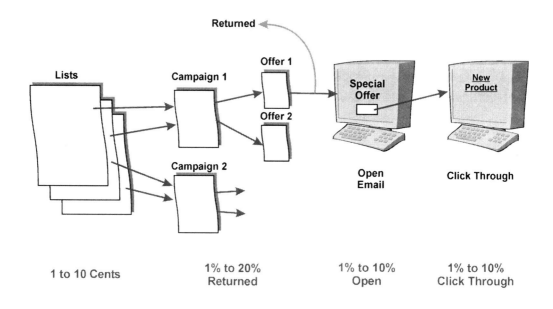

Figure 1.15, Email Marketing Metrics

Email marketing starts with the gathering or renting of lists. Promotional campaigns are created that use these lists to send promotional offers via email broadcast systems. Email broadcast systems usually contain features that allow for the tracking of the results of email marketing programs.

Figure 1.15 shows an example of an email marketing process with some sample numbers. This example shows that email marketing is the process of managing lists, developing ad campaigns, creating promotional offers, broadcasting email messages and tracking the results. This diagram shows an example of lists that cost 1 to 10 cents per name. Names in these lists are grouped to match specific marketing campaigns. These marketing campaigns have several promotional offers. The emails are broadcasted and some of the emails are returned(1% to 20% returns are typical). Some of the emails that make it to the recipient are never opened. Of the 25% to 80% of the emails that are opened, approximately 2% to 10% click through to the specific product or service order page.

Email Lists

Email lists are groups of emails (called list "subscribers") that are owned or rented. Email address acquisition is the process of adding email addresses and their related data to a list. Email address acquisition processes can range from asking customers for the email address when they visit a store to using newsletters and other promotional programs to get people to register their email addresses.

Companies typically have more than one list or they categorize their list into multiple segments. Email lists are commonly managed by list server companies. These companies specialize in storing, sorting, broadcasting and tracking email marketing programs.

Adding people to a list may be performed by an option-in (opt-in) or option out (opt-out) system. Option-in is a process that requires a person to agree (select an option) to be added to a list. Opt-out is the declining of an option (option out) for a process such as to be included on a mailing list or subscription service. Opt-in lists are usually more valuable because users have had to read and select the opt-in to the list.

To help ensure or validate that people have chosen to be added to a list, confirmed opt-in or double opt-in may be used. Confirmed opt-in is an email address or list of email addresses where each of the listed email addresses has responded to an email message or via other communication means that they agree to be included in a mailing list. Double opt-in is a process that requires that a person agree (select an option) to be added to a list and to confirm to a second validation option such as an email confirmation.

Email lists may be purchased or rented from the company that owns the list or via a list broker. A list broker is a person or company who rents or sells lists of prospects for marketing purposes (such as direct mail campaigns). When acquiring lists, you should check to ensure that the seller is authorized to sell names.

List brokers specialize in finding lists and negotiating list rental agreements. The list broker is commonly paid a commission by the list seller. Email lists can be filtered (called "selects") for key characteristics to help target them to customer needs or desires.

Another way to get access to lists is list swapping. List swapping is an agreement by two (or more) companies to provide access to their list in exchange for access to the other company's list. List swapping may be a simple agreement that requires each list owner to broadcast the promotional offer or it may involve the use of a third party list management company. When the list size is different, portions of lists may be used or the company that has a smaller list may allow multiple broadcasts of their list at different times in exchange for access to the larger list.

Email List Sources

Email lists may be acquired by developing subscription lists, or buying or renting contact information from other companies or list brokers. Common sources of lists include magazines, trade shows, associations, and companies. List brokers can be used to find list providers or users.

To help control the distribution of lists, it is common for list owners to plant (seed) names into their lists to see who and how many times a list has been used. The list may be made available to approved mail houses or list management companies to ensure the list renter does not gain direct access to the list.

Magazines

Industry magazines are a common source of qualified email lists as the readers are professionals that share common interests. In addition to renting the list from a magazine, the magazine has a relationship with the reader which may assist in the willingness of the recipient to receive and open the email.

Trade Shows

Trade shows commonly provide or rent lists to exhibitors of the trade shows. To encourage vendors to exhibit, trade shows may restrict the sale of lists to companies that are exhibiting at the trade show. Vendors who exhibit at the trade shows may capture contact information for list building via badge reader devices.

Associations

Associations may provide access to member lists. The members of an association may be regulatory managers that are not directly involved with the direct implementation or purchase of products or services.

Companies

Companies may sell, swap or provide access to customer or prospect lists. As part of the list agreement, companies may also agree to provide or to allow the use of an introductory letter to add credibility to the sender of the email.

List Brokers

A list broker is a person or company who rents or sells lists of prospects for marketing purposes. List brokers are typically paid a commission of approximately 20% by the list owner.

List Management

List management is the acquiring, sending and updating of lists of people or companies that share common interests. Lists are commonly managed in list servers.

List Server

A list server is a computer or a company service that can distribute and track the delivery of lists of email addresses associated with specific categories and marketing campaigns. List servers allow users to import, process, or export lists from data files such as text (CSV), spreadsheet (excel) or other format that can identify each email address (person) and their related data.

List Importing

List importing is the process of transferring a list of subscribers and their associated fields (such as name, address and date subscribed) into a data table. List importing may involve the adding, overwriting or merging of new data with existing data.

A list is composed of subscribers (records) and fields (items). Fields typically have labels (names) of the data types they hold (such as L_name for last name). Subscriber information can be manually entered or imported from other data sources (such as existing customer lists). When data is imported from other sources, the fields between the data file and the list must be mapped. Field mapping is used to adapt or change the field names or data formats between data files. An example of field mapping is the assigning of the field labeled First_Name in data table 1 to the field labeled F_Name in data table 2.

A common data file format used by list servers is comma separated value (CSV). The CSV file structure separates information into records (lines) and items (fields) with the fields separated by commas. Data files in other formats (such as Excel or other types of databases) can be typically exported to CSV format.

The first row in a data file may contain the names of the data elements (the field list) for each person (the record). Choosing names that reflect their content simplifies the importing into list servers.

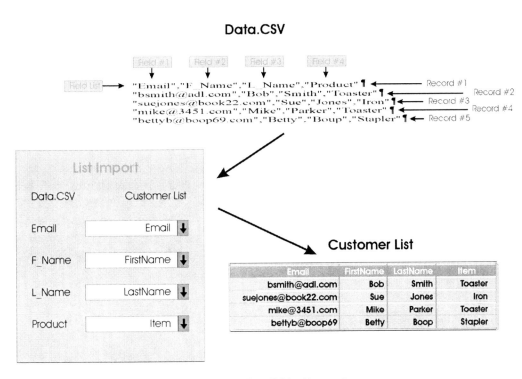

Figure 1.16, Email List Importing

Importing subscribers into list management programs involves selecting the data file source, selecting the data format (such as CSV) and mapping the data file files into the list fields. The list server software may have the ability to automatically detect and possibly suggest the fields it thinks match the list with the data file.

Figure 1.16 shows the how a list can be imported to a list server. This list server is importing from a CSV text file, which has been mapped into the list format. The data file contains multiple subscribers (records) with fields named Email (email address), F_name (first name), L_name (last name) and product. Each line of the CSV file (lines end with a paragraph mark) is a record and the names of each field are stored in the first record of the CSV data file. The user has required the incoming data fields to be mapped to the list fields; Email to Email, F_name to FirstName, L_name to LastName and Product to Item.

After a list is imported, a list server may create an import error report. The error report contains information that identifies and potentially summarizes (e.g. total number of errors) which records or data could not be transferred into a file or database. This could include subscriber records that could not be imported because there was missing information or invalid formats.

Due to Internet regulations, companies can receive significant penalties for the transmission of SPAM emails and list management companies can be responsible for these fines if they assist in spamming. List server companies often require proof of list validity before they allow list broadcasting. Be prepared to provide information or links to subscription pages to the list management company after you import your list to validate that your list was acquired in a legitimate way.

Campaign Management

Campaign management is the process of identifying, scheduling and tracking the marketing communication activities associated with marketing projects as the project scope is defined. Campaigns involve the selection of lists or audiences, creation of offers and potentially the personalization of the offers.

Audiences

Audiences are groups of people on one or more lists that share common characteristics. Audience types can include previous buyers of certain types of products, people from certain age groups, or people that have purchased multiple times.

Audiences can be defined to allow for better targeting of promotional campaigns. For example, audiences that have been repeat buyers may be offered a reward gift that is similar in category to the products that they have previously purchased.

Email Offers

An email offer is a promotion of a product or service that is sent by email. Email offers contain a description of the item(s) being offered along with the details and terms of the offer. Important parts of email offers include the subject line, lead paragraph, ad copy and a call to action.

Subject line

A subject line is a portion of an email that provides preview information to the recipient about the email. The recipient usually views the subject line before they open the email.

The purpose of the subject line for an email offer is to get the recipient to open the email. The subject line should focus on the need or benefit for the product or service that is being offered rather than the product details. For example, people are likely to be more interested in how their mobile phone can be used as a family photo album rather than the model ABX-220 is 40% discounted.

Subject lines tend to have a limited number of characters that can be displayed to the user so the most important words should be contained within the first 40 to 50 characters. The use of certain words in the subject line may trigger a spam filter. For example, the use of the words "Free" or "Trial" may automatically get the recipient's email discarded by their SPAM filter.

Lead Paragraph

A lead paragraph is the first paragraph of the content part of a media item (such as an email message) that is read or seen by the recipient. The lead paragraph usually focuses on the key interest area and sets the tone of the item or message. The purpose of the lead paragraph is to get the recipient to want to read the rest of the email.

Ad Content

Ad content is the text and media portions of an ad. Ad content can include pictures, audio and video clips, all of which will enhance the effectiveness of the promotional message. Ad content should be structured in a way to get the recipient's attention (opening statement), interest (matching what they are looking for), give conviction (they need to believe what you are offering can help them), desire (build the motivation to use or want what you have to offer) and define what they should do (what action they should take to satisfy their needs).

Call to Action

A call to action is a specific task or process that is requested from a person who has received or is viewing an advertising message.

Email Templates

An email template is a set of email messages that contain structural components and media elements (such as page banners). Email templates for email marketing campaigns typically include a single product page, multiple product promotion, newsletter and other common promotional message types that allow the user to quickly modify and produce new email mes-

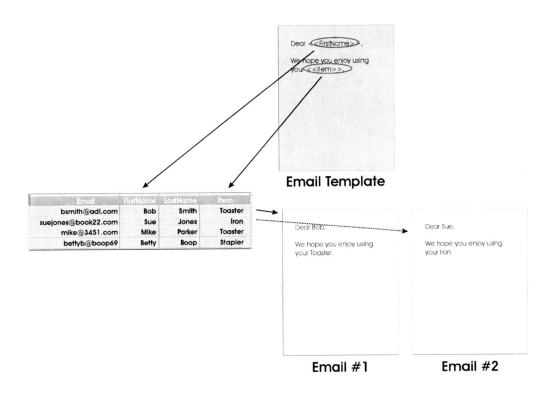

Figure 1.17, Email Personalization

sages.

Email Personalization

Email personalization is the process of modifying email content to better match the personal interests of the intended recipient. Email management systems may allow email messages to be personalized through the insertion of fields (value tags). Field tags are inserted into the text of an email message which is replaced from data in the fields of the subscriber list.

Figure 1.17 shows how emails can be personalized. This email message has been personalized by adding name and product fields to the email template. This example shows that the field names in the email message are surrounded by double brackets and the field names are contained in a spreadsheet. When the list server processes the email, it detects the field in the email and substitutes it with the field data from the record for which the email is created.

Email Format Types

Email formats are the structure of the media components that can be sent to email recipients. Email format types include text, HTML and multipart.

Text Format

Text format is a document or message that contains a standard set of characters along with a limited set of formatting characters such as carriage return and line feed. Some email programs cannot or do not accept rich media components (e.g. pictures or video clips). To reach these recipients, text only email formats should be used.

Format	Appearance	Notes
Text	Plain text.	Can be delivered to all types of email programs and basically looks the same to all recipients.
HTML	Graphics and Text with Formatting	High impact graphics can be used. May not be deliverable to all recipients.
Multipart	Text or HTML	Text or HTML sent based on the capabilities of the recipients email program.

Figure 1.18, Email Formats

HTML Format

HTML format emails can contain formatting information along with the ability to display and include links and media items such as pictures, audio and video clips. HTML emails can contain highly motivational rich media content.

Multipart Format

Multipart format is a document or message that is available in both HTML and text formats. The selection of the text or HTML part may be made based on the detection of the capability of the recipient's presentation or email program.

Figure 1.18 shows the different format types available for email messages. This table shows that email messages may be in text, HTML, Multipart formats. The text format can be opened by all recipients who use email. The HTML format requires that the recipient can receive and process graphics and other forms of rich media. The multipart format is used for either HTML or text dependent on the capabilities of the recipients email program.

Email Broadcasting

Email broadcasting is the transmission of promotional materials (text or graphics) that are sent via email transmission. Email broadcasting involves selecting which campaign is to be sent and when its transmission will be initiated. Once the campaign and list have been selected, some of the transmissions may be removed by suppression lists. The broadcasts may be scheduled to be sent at times that are better suited to the recipients (during the weekdays).

List Suppression

A suppression list of is a group of mailing addresses (usually an email list) that will be used to stop the sending of marketing or other materials from a marketing campaign. A suppression list usually consists of people who have requested not to receive additional marketing contacts from a company or organization. Suppression list options may include the restriction of emails based on email addresses, domain names or a combination of the two.

Suppression lists may include house file list. House file suppression is the use of a list of people who are already receiving promotional information

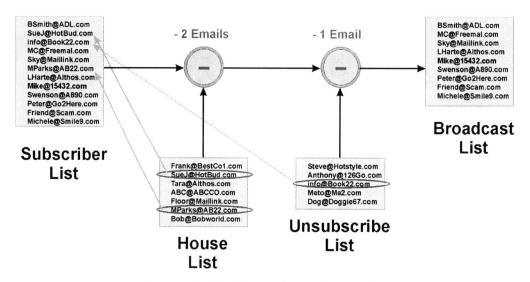

Figure 1.19, Email List Address Suppression

from a company to suppress the sending of additional (duplicated) emails to that person.

An unsubscribe list contains email addresses of people who have requested to be removed from a mailing list.

A domain name suppression list contains web addresses that should not receive emails from your broadcast. A domain name suppression list may be used to suppress emails that might be sent to the domain names of competing companies. The inclusion of a domain name stops the sending of any email in your list that contains that domain name.

Figure 1.19 shows how email address suppression can be used to disable or remove email addresses from an email list. This diagram shows that a master email list is filtered using both a house file suppression list and unsubscribe email list. Email address matches found in either of these lists disables or removes the names from the email broadcast.

Broadcast Scheduling

Email broadcast scheduling is the process of selecting campaigns or content and establishing a time that the emails will be transmitted. It is preferable to send email broadcasts at times when people are not overwhelmed. It is often good to send broadcasts in the late morning or early afternoon and to avoid sending broadcasts on weekends, Mondays or Fridays.

List management services may have an option to immediately send an email ("send now"). If you use a send now feature, it can take some time for the email to be broadcasted as the server may be busy with many other email broadcasts. This may result in your email being received outside your desired reception time period.

Email Reports

An email report is the analysis and presentation of email delivery status. This typically includes how many total emails were sent, how many were returned (bounces), how many were opened, and what links were clicked in the email.

Delivery Attempts

Delivery attempts are the total number of messages that were transmitted as part of a marketing campaign (such as an email campaign). Delivery attempts are the number of emails that were actually transmitted after all the suppressions that are applied to the list.

Suppressions are the number of messages (such as email messages) that were stopped due to the matching criteria in a suppression list. A suppression list may contain email address, domain names or other criteria that is used to block the sending of emails in a list. In some cases, a suppression list is provided by a company that is renting a list as a way to stop emails from being sent to their existing customers or to keep emails from being sent to their competitors.

Email Bounces

An email bounce is the return of an e-mail message to its original sender due to the inability of an email system to accept and deliver the message. A bounced message may be returned for significant (user not registered), temporary or less significant reasons (mailbox full).

Email broadcast systems may classify returned email messages into hard bounce and soft bounce types. A hard bounce is an email was returned because the address was not valid and is not deliverable (possibly a fake email address). A soft bounce has occurred when an email was returned for some reason other than the address was not deliverable. List management systems may disable the sending of messages to an email address after a defined number of attempted deliveries.

Disables

Disables are the number of subscriber records in a list that have been disabled from broadcasts. Disables may result from the inability of a list management system to successfully deliver messages to the recipient.

Unsubscribes

Unsubscribes are the number of recipients in a list who have selected the option to have their name removed or disabled from future mailings.

Successful Deliveries

Successful deliveries are the number of emails that reached their destination reduced by the number of disabling responses (such as unsubscribes). The number of successful deliveries does not necessarily mean the number of people who have seen the incoming subject line. It may have been received by some email systems and filtered by a SPAM filter.

Email Opens

Email opens is the number of people who have selected and opened emails so the contents can be displayed. The number of email opens may be classified into categories such as total opens and unique email opens.

Total opens are the number of times a message is opened by all the recipients of a campaign. Total opens include repeated opens by the same person. Email open rate is a measure of the people who receive and open an email to the total number of people who have received the email. Some reports show a change in open rate status since previous broadcasts to allow a marketing manager to determine if new campaigns are more or less effective than previous campaigns.

Unique email opens are the number of email messages that have been opened by identifiable recipients. Unique email opens exclude the counting of email opens when the same recipient opens the same email multiple times.

Estimated opens are the number of email messages that are estimated to have been opened by recipients where direct tracking is not an option. Estimated opens may be calculated for text based email messages using the measurements of HTML version of the same email.

Click Tracking

Click tracking is the process of counting or gathering information about the selection or use of web links. A tracked click through is the selection of a link by a web site visitor or email recipient, which can be counted or has other measurable attributes. The link is made trackable by adding a campaign tracking code to the end of the hyperlink. Click tracking enables the measurement of total and unique clicks.

Total clicks is the number of times links in a message have been selected by all recipients of an email campaign. Unique clicks is the number of times links in a message have been selected by each recipient of a campaign. Unique clicks only counts one click per link by the same person.

Click rate is the ratio of how many times a link within a message is clicked (selected) as compared to the number of time it is opened or viewed. Click rate is also called click-through rate (CTR).

Complaints

Delivery Results	Totals	Rate
Attempts	2700	
Suppressions	0	0
Bounces	92	3.4%
Disables	7	0.3%
Unsubscribes	1	0.04%
Successful Deliveries	**2600**	**96.3%**
Total Opens	390	15%
Unique Opens	270	10%
Total Clicks	130	5%
Unique Clicks	104	4%

Figure 1.20, Email Campaign Measurement

Email complaints are the reporting to a service (such as an email provider) that unwanted messages or media items have been received. An excessive number of complaints may result in the blocking or disabling of an email list server.

Forward to a Friend

Forward to a friend is a hyperlink that is included in an email message that enables and encourages the recipient to forward the message to a friend.

Figure 1.20 shows how email marketing campaigns can be measured. This diagram shows a campaign where 2700 emails that were selected to be sent to recipients (delivery attempts). Of these, 92 were returned as undeliverable (bounces) and 7 were undeliverable for permanent reasons (disables). Of the 2600 successful deliveries, 390 emails were opened (15%). Of all the emails opened, 270 were opened by unique people (10%). There were 130 total clicks (5%) and of these, 104 were unique clicks (4%).

Autoresponders

Autoresponders are software programs that automatically create response messages when incoming messages are received. Autoresponder capabilities vary from simple responses to incoming email messages such as "I'm currently out of the office, will be back," to personalized letters such as "Dear Tom, Thanks for requesting more information on our ABC product, from the information you gave use, we...".

Autoresponders can be an effective tool to immediately provide information to people who request information of a specific type (e.g. send an email to "moreinfo@althos.com"). Autoresponders can also be setup to delay their response to provide follow-up communication. Autoresponder event delays may be used to provide a person or information submitter with a time gap to develop a better understanding of their need (anticipation) before receiving a response or promotional message.

Affiliate Marketing

Affiliate marketing is the process of sharing marketing and sales programs between companies that want to sell products (merchants) through other companies (affiliates) that are willing to promote these products to their customers. The affiliate merchant compensates the affiliate partners for their role in communicating and selling to customers.

Affiliate programs are commonly setup as pay for performance programs, which allows the merchant to control their marketing costs as promotional costs only occur when sales or controllable actions occur. Affiliate programs can produce higher advertising revenue for promotional partners as the affiliate commission can be much higher than advertising revenue that is received from other types of advertising (such as banner ads). The typical ad revenue for banner and other ads is approximately $10 to $20 per thousand unique visitors. The revenue from affiliate links may generate over $100 per thousand visitors.

For affiliate marketing to work, a company that has a marketing interest that is similar to that of another company makes contact to propose a shared marketing relationship. The affiliate partner (also called a publisher) may promote the products or services on their web site, by sending email messages, using search engine marketing programs or other forms of communication to potential customers. The affiliate merchant provides the affiliate partner with content (such as product images and descriptions) to use in their promotional programs.

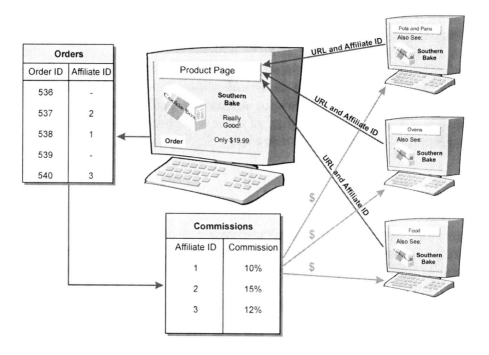

Figure 1.21, Affiliate Link Operation

After the terms of the affiliate relationship are negotiated, an affiliate marketing link account is created and hyperlinks with account codes are provided to the affiliate partner. An additional link and login account may be created to provide the company or person with a link that can be used to track the referred sales activity of the affiliate partner.

Figure 1.21 shows the basic operation of affiliate links. This example shows that affiliate links are provided to affiliate marketing partners and these links are inserted on pages that have a common interest with the affiliate's product. When the affiliate web sites' visitors click on the affiliate link, this link provides the web address of the destination page along with an affiliate ID code. When the destination page is accessed, the affiliate ID code is stored during the visitor's session. If the visitor purchases a product, the affiliate ID is stored along with the order information. This order information and affiliate commission table are used to calculate the commissions that are paid to the affiliate partner.

Affiliate Types

Affiliate partners may promote on web sites (web portals) or by email marketing, search engine marketing or other media communication options.

Web Portals

Web portals are Internet web sites that act as an interface between a user and an information service. Web portals commonly contain specialized content or specific functions that serve users who share a common interest. Examples of web portals include magazines, associations, industry directories and online dictionaries.

Email Marketers

Email marketers send marketing and sales information using email messaging systems. Email marketing systems generally combine advanced message broadcast systems along with tracking systems that can monitor the reception, opening and response to email messages that have been sent. Examples of email marketing can include sending promotional messages to subscribers of newsletters, magazines and other industry lists.

Search Engine Marketers

Search engine marketing is the process of promoting products or services using the listing results of search engines. SEM may use a combination of paid and unpaid listings or ads that are presented by search engines. SEM's may use paid advertising (adword) campaigns to promote the products or services of affiliate merchants.

Blog Marketers

Blog marketing is the process of inserting promotional messages into blog postings. Blog marketers may disguise the promotional content as referring to solutions or subjects that are of interest to blog visitors.

Affiliate Networks

Affiliate networks are companies or systems that link merchants that want to promote their products or services to companies that are willing to promote these products or services on their web sites on a performance (usually revenue sharing) basis. Affiliate networks enable companies to participate in affiliate marketing without the need to directly contact or make relationships with other companies. An example of an affiliate network is www.doubleclick.com.

Affiliate networks provide the opportunity for merchants to promote their products or services on hundreds or thousands of web sites. Affiliate networks also allow web site owners (promoters) to sell advertising space to many companies. Merchants and promoters join the network, classify their products or web pages according to categories, and the affiliate network begins to distribute ads from merchants to web sites.

Because affiliate networks can isolate merchants from promoters, affiliate network systems may require the review and approval of merchants and vendors prior to authorizing participation in the affiliate network.

What Affiliates Want

Ideally affiliates want long-term business relationships that pay high commissions compared to other affiliate programs, have a limited number of competing affiliates, a good supply of compelling media and content, training about the products and promotion, and campaigns with lots of new products to offer.

Long Term Relationship

Affiliate agreements often have terms of several years with automatic renewal options. It takes time for affiliate partners to research and setup affiliate relationships so they look for businesses with products and partners that have the potential for multi-year relationships.

Competitive Commission Rates

Commission rates for affiliate agreements are often composed of a mix of compensation that is paid for clicks, leads and sales. Affiliates look for partners with commission structures that are comparable to other companies of similar types. However, affiliates may be willing to accept reduced commissions for better support and a bigger mix of products that they can sell.

Limited Number of Affiliates

Affiliate partners compete with other affiliate partners so affiliate programs that limit the number of affiliate partners have a higher value to the affiliate marketing partner.

Marketing Materials

Marketing materials are items or media that can be provided to people or potential customers to promote action (such as buying products or services). Affiliate partners commonly desire to use online media centers to obtain media items such as product photos, descriptions and other media objects they can use for online and other forms of media.

Training and Support

Affiliates need to learn about products and services to effectively market them. While many of their initial questions may be answered in a FAQ web page, affiliates can significantly benefit from tutorials, web seminars and other forms of training and support.

Good Sales Reporting

Affiliates desire to have sales reports that detail both marketing and sales activities that are related to their marketing programs such as the number of clicks, leads and sales generated.

Wide Product Selection

Affiliates desire to have access to a wide variety of products and services to sell so they can group and offer these items in unique combinations or in targeted promotional offers.

New Content and Offers

Affiliates desire to have early access to new offers and promotional opportunities as a way for them to get competitive advantages.

Affiliate Marketing Challenges

Affiliate marketing partners compete to obtain and keep customers. As a result, affiliate partners may take aggressive measures to improve their promotional performance. These tactics or processes may not be in the best interest of the affiliate merchant. Some possible challenges include changing the promotional message, associating the product with other products or services and misrepresenting the offer or terms of the offer.

Change of Promotional Messages

Affiliates may modify the content of promotional graphics or offers to better appeal to the audiences they reach. While this may be desirable because affiliate marketing partners may know their audience better than the producer of the product or service, the change of promotional message may result in unwanted messages being interpreted by end customers.

Brand or Product Association

Brand or product association is the linking or asserting the relationship of a brand or product with other brands or products. Brand or product association may occur when a logo or product is located on the same web page or near another logo or brand that is on the web page. Affiliate merchants may define how media may be used or positioned on web sites and other promotional brochures.

Misrepresentation

Affiliate marketing partners may overstate features or benefits in order to motivate customers to purchase products or services. This could include adding performance guarantees, features or using distorted or incorrect product photos.

Affiliate Reporting

Affiliate reporting is the providing of data in a format that indicates sales activities that are related to specific criteria such as the particular sales channel or person who is responsible for the sales. Affiliates desire to have sales reports that detail both marketing and sales activities that are related to their marketing programs such as the number of clicks, leads and sales generated.

Search Engine Optimization (SEO)

Search engine optimization (SEO) is the design and modification of web sites to allow search engines to more easily identify and prioritize (rank higher) the display in the search results window. The higher a link appears in a search results list, the larger the number of viewers and the higher the potential number of web visitors.

Figure 1.22, Search Engine Organic Optimization

To list web sites (URLs) in the results of searches, search engines must first discover the existence of the web page and include the discovery in its search index file. Link discovery may be performed by directly submitting to search engines or through the use of web spiders that discover a new web page by following links from other pages it has already indexed.

After a search engine has identified a link, it must categorize the link and associate the link with keywords or subjects. It may do this using a variety of ranking criteria such as using content within the page (keywords), using site descriptive data (metadata), related web pages (linked web pages) or other criteria.

Figure 1.22 shows how search engine optimization page ranking can be influenced by various factors. These include the number keywords in the web page (keyword density), the number of links from related web sites (inbound links), the type and amount of content on the web page and how well the keywords match the search criteria.

In addition to general web search engines (such as Google, Yahoo, and MSN), there are other types of specialty search engines, which include comparison shopping search engines (CSSE), directory search engines and niche portal search engines.

Listing Types

Search results can be displayed in various formats including organic listings, sponsored links, pay for placement and trusted feed.

Organic Listing

Organic listings (also called "natural listings") are a list of web pages (URL Addresses) that are produced as a result of a search engine process. Organic search results are a list of web sites that are displayed as a result of searching for keywords where the matches are not directly paid (supposed to occur without bias).

Sponsored Link

Sponsored search results are a list of web site links that are displayed as a result of searching for keywords where the matches are paid (such as pay per click). Sponsored links are usually displayed in a special sponsored area (such as on top or on the right side of the display), which indicates the links are sponsored.

Pay for Placement (PFP)

Pay for placement is a marketing program that allows advertisers to pay for listings in list response of search engines. Pay for placement programs guarantee that listings will be included in the organic search results. Even though a company pays to include the link in the search results, this listing does not indicate it is a sponsored link.

Trusted Feed

Trusted feed is a paid advertising inclusion program that guarantees the search engine listing of web site URLs. Trusted feed does not guarantee the ranking position of the listing.

Search Engine Ranking Criteria

Search engines periodically search through web pages or data records to find matches to specific words or items to create a search engine index. The search engine uses the index to find matches to key words (search words) to people enter to find related web pages. When the search engine creates the index, it uses various criteria to relate or rank the index to key search words. Ranking criteria may include; metadata, keywords in the content, content value, inbound link popularity and keyword emphasis. Ranking criteria changes over time as marketing companies discover how to optimize their listings in search engines.

Metadata

Web site metadata is information that describes the contents or focus of the web page that is created by the web site developer. Search engines may use metadata to categorize the web site. Some of the metadata (such as the title) may be displayed in the search results window.

Keyword Density

Keyword density is the number of times a keyword appears versus the other words on a web page. Keyword density is a major component of most search engines algorithms. A good keyword density can range from 2% to 6% depending on the search engine or other ranking program.

Some search engines penalize the ranking of web pages when they determine that keyword stuffing has been used. Keyword stuffing is the adding of keywords into the content of web pages to help increase the relative ranking of a web page by search engines.

Inbound Link Popularity

Link popularity is a measure of the interest that users have in finding a link (URL). Search engines use link popularity as a factor in determining the relative ranking of web page URLs that are presented as the result of a keyword search. It is important to get inbound links from popular web sites that have content that is similar or related to the web page.

Keyword Positioning

Keyword positioning is the locating of key words within a web page or document to gain recognition or emphasis value. An example of keyword positioning is the locating of keywords in titles, headings or at the beginning of a web page.

Content Value

Content value is a measure of the contents of a document or web page as it relates to a category or interest of a content user. Some of the ways to assign value to content include how much content along with the structure and relationship of key words within the content.

Duplicate content is data or media that are the same on other web pages. Search engines may reduce the ranking (create a penalty) for sites that contain the same or very similar content.

Keyword Emphasis

Keyword emphasis is the use of special attributes such as bolding or using keywords in a heading style.

Search Engine Link Submission

Search engine submission is the process of providing information to a search engine (or the company that manages the search engine) so that it can be added to their list of available sites that will be displayed when users search for information.

Manual Submission

Manual submission is the process of updating a service (such as a search engine) through a process that requires the individual submission of data (such as completing an online form).

Automatic Submission

Automatic submission is the process of updating a service (such as a search engine) through a process that allows for the unassisted transfer of existing information (such as a form that has been previously completed).

A web spider is an Internet search engine software application that automatically finds and collects information about web sites. If you include a link to new web pages in web pages that are already indexed by search engines, the search engine will likely automatically add the new page to its index.

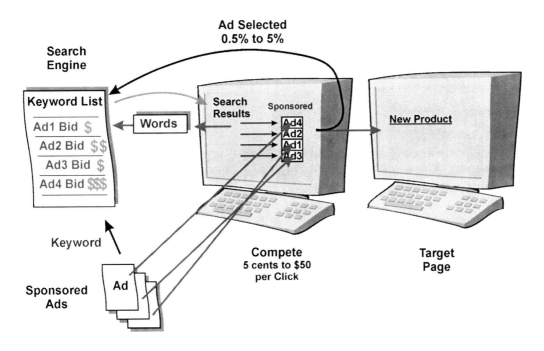

Figure 1.23, Adword Marketing

Adword Marketing

Adword marketing is a process that uses key words (keywords) that potential customers enter into search engines to find product or service information where the results of their search also show paid advertising messages. To perform adword marketing, a list of keywords is created and associated with a URL along with a short message to accompany the listing. When the search term(s) matches the keyword, the ad is displayed under sponsored listings.

Figure 1.23 shows the basic keyword advertising process. In this example, four companies have submitted ads to search engines that match a keyword. When an Internet user enters a search word into the search engine, the search engine provides the user with a list of URLs found along with a list of sponsored ads. The sponsored ad presentation (impressions) is organized with the highest bid on top and ads with lower bids positioned lower on the screen.

Keyword Ads

Keyword ads are communication messages that appear as a result of a keyword match. Keyword ads may be text ads, image ads or video ads. In 2008, the most common forms of keyword ads were text ads.

Keyword Text Ad Structure

Keyword text ad structure is the promotional message that is composed by the words and their position. Text ads contain an ad title, description and displayed web address (display URL). The title is usually selectable (clickable) and will redirect the display to a new web page (not necessarily to the displayed web link).

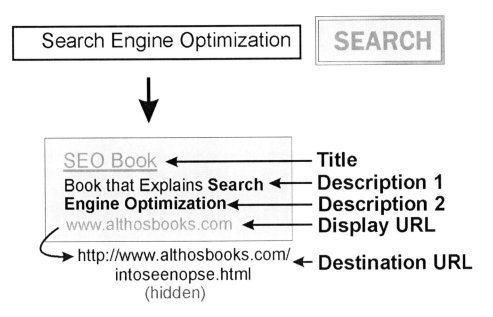

The title line is usually emphasized (bolded an underlined) so the title words should be chosen to get the attention of the viewer. The description contains words that should be of interest to the viewer and encourage them to click the ad (a call to action). The description may be 1 or 2 lines and the actual display of the text ad description may be shortened by the browser window or when the ad is displayed on the web page of search engine partner sites. The keywords that matched the person's search may be displayed boldly in the text ad. Some systems allow for the insertion of search words into the text ad, which can better target the viewer's interest.

A display URL is the web address that is shown to the web site visitor. A display URL may have a limited number of characters and it is commonly the home web page address. A destination URL is the web address that is used when a web site visitor selects a link. A destination URL may include a web page address and additional criteria such as a product code or other attributes.

Figure 1.24 shows the typical structure of a keyword ad. A pay per click ad that is composed of a title (emphasized), description (1 or 2 lines), a displayed URL (web address) and a destination URL. This example also shows that this pay per click ad bolds the search words in the ad.

Ad Approval

Ads for adword marketing programs usually require approval from the search marketing company. Ad approval is the process of reviewing the content of an advertising message to ensure it meets legal and/or advertising company guidelines. In some cases, ads may be allowed to display during the approval process.

Ad Variations

Ad variations are advertising messages that are expressed in different ways. Ad variations may be rotated to determine which ad variation has the best marketing pull. Some search marketing programs allow for automatic ad rotation or optimized ad rotations, which allows the ads with the best performance (best pull) to be displayed more often.

Keyword Selection

Keyword selection is the process of identifying and selecting words or word sequences that match what potential customers are looking for.

Brainstorming

Keywords may be selected through the process of brainstorming with industry experts (the product manager) on words that relate to their product or service or keyword tools may be used to search through web pages or other content to identify potential keywords.

Keyword Selection Tool

A keyword selection tool is a program software application feature that can be used to select keywords in a keyword marketing program (adwords) that are likely to achieve desired marketing objectives such as the number of words matched and selected. Some search engine marketing companies offer free keyword selection tools that look for related search words.

Keyword Combinations

Keyword combinations are sequences of words that are used to better match search terms. Keyword combinations can be used to better qualify the meaning of what searchers are looking for.

Keyword Variations

Keyword variations are the use of tense, plurality, misspellings and other potential changes to keywords that people may use in searches.

Keyword Groups

A keyword group is a set of keywords that share some commonality such as industry or product type.

Keyword Matching

For adword marketing campaigns, ads are displayed when user search words and advertiser keywords match. Keyword matching is a process of comparing search words to keyword listings for advertising messages to determine which advertising messages match the search criteria.

Keyword matching options may include exact match (identical search words and keyword), phrase match (word sequences are located within the search words), broad match (the words located anywhere in the search words), context match (words match that have similar meanings) and negative matching (words that inhibit the display of ads).

In general, the number of impressions decreases as the keyword matching becomes more precise. However, the more precise the matching, the higher the conversion rate tends to be.

Exact Matching

Exact matching is the process of comparing search words to other keywords to determine if they match exactly. Exact matches are usually not case sensitive but it may be possible to set them up to be case sensitive.

Phrase Matching

A phrase match is a comparison between a reference (such as a keyword) and another item (such as search words) where the exact sequence of the phrase is located within the search words. A phrase match is commonly indicated by the inclusion of quote marks around the search words and/or keywords.

Broad Matching

Broad keyword matching is when one or more of the keywords match in any area or sequence.

Context Matching

Match Type	Description
Exact	Each character must match may be case sensitive
Phrase	The exact sequence of the phrase is located within the search words
Broad	Search words can appear anywhere and in any position
Context	Words must have similar meanings
Negative	Stops ad display for specific (negative) words

Figure 1.25, Keyword Matching Options

A context match is a comparison between a reference (such as a keyword) and another item (such as a search word) where the meanings of the two items match. The search word "car" and the keyword "auto" would be a context match.

Negative Matching

Negative keywords are identifying words or terms that are used to suppress the results or matching items of a search. Negative keywords can be used in combination with keywords to better define desired matching results where a broad keyword match may include unwanted results. An example of a negative keyword is to stop the display of ads when the searcher uses the word "Free" in their search words.

Figure 1.25 shows some of the keyword matching options. This example shows that keyword matching options may include exact matching, phrase matching, broad matching and negative matching. Exact matching requires that the exact sequence of characters (and possibly the same case) must occur for a match. Phrase matching requires a sequence of words to appear in the text. Broad or context matching allows some or all of the words to occur for a match to occur. Negative matching removes a match if a negative word is found.

Keyword Bidding

Keyword bidding is the process of assigning bid amounts that pertain to a specific advertising message that is associated with a key word that will be used in a search process. When the keyword criteria is matched (such as matching a search word in an online search), the bid amounts are reviewed and the highest bids are selected. The advertising message(s) are then dis-

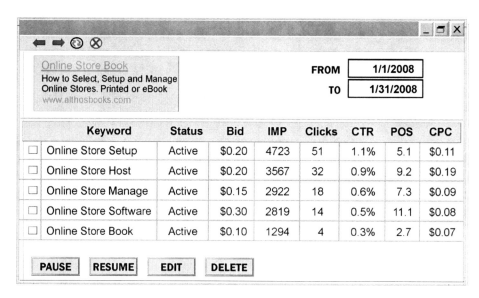

Figure 1.26, Keyword Groups

played in the order of bid amount.

Keyword bidding campaigns may use the next lowest bid amount to determine the actual bid cost. This means that the click cost will typically be lower than the bid amount.

Keyword bidding systems may allow for the setting of a maximum advertising cost per day per campaign. Because it is possible to select a keyword that has multiple meanings which can be very popular, setting maximum advertising budgets per campaign is usually a wise choice.

Figure 1.26 shows how adword marketing can use keyword bidding to control the display of adword ads. This example shows that a bid can be assigned to each keyword and that ad display impressions (IMP) for each keyword can vary (based on keyword popularity and bid amount). This keyword bidding system shows the number of clicks that resulted from adword ad displays and their resulting click through rate (CTR). The average position (POS) of the ad is provided to help the adword advertiser choose where their ad is positioned relative to other advertisers (higher numbers mean the ad is lower on the page or on a separate page). The actual cost per click (CPC) is provided to show the actual advertising costs for each keyword (usually lower than the bid amount).

Affiliate Search Networks

Affiliate search networks are systems that can place adword ads on web pages other than that of the search engine company. Search engines may call affiliate search networks by other names such as "content network".

The affiliate search partner that displays the ads receives compensation when the ads are selected. Although the potential for better matching ads with content exists, the use of affiliate networks can have reduced ad performance. In particular, affiliate search partners may have higher ad impressions and lower conversion (actual buyers) resulting in a higher cost of marketing.

To compensate for this, search engine companies may allow the advertiser to enter different bid amounts for the search network and the affiliate or

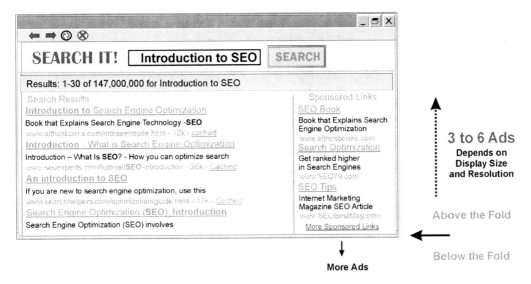

Figure 1.27, Keyword Ad Positioning

content network. If you allow ads to be placed on affiliate search networks, bidding lower amounts on the affiliate network is reccommended until marketing performance rates can be determined.

Ad Positioning

Adword ad positioning is the selection of a location of an ad on a media item or rank on a series of ads. The first position in a sequence of ads may have the highest click through while lower position ads tend to have higher conversion rates.

People who are purchasing products are likely to look through multiple ads and they are not as likely to return to the first ad they selected (the top ad). It is possible that increasing the keyword bid to increase the search position can reduce the performance of the advertising program.

Figure 1.27 shows how keyword ad positioning can influence the effectiveness of adword marketing campaigns. This diagram shows that adword listings that appear higher on the display tend to get more clicks. This example shows that 3 to 6 ads may appear on the initial search results page and the number of ads that display depends on the display size and resolution settings. The searcher may select to view additional ads that are located below the fold.

Click Fraud

Click fraud is the selection of links ("clicks") by users who do not have an interest in using the link for its intended purpose. Click fraud may result from users who receive compensation for link clicks on their web sites or web sites they manage from advertisers. Click fraud estimates range from below

10% to more than 70%.

Accidental Click Fraud

Accidental click fraud is the selection of links ("clicks") by users for a purpose other than its intended purpose without the intent of defrauding the system or for monetary gains. This can occur if a user is rapidly navigating through a web page and accidentally clicks on a link. Unfortunately, accidental click fraud tends to happen more often with ads that are displayed on top (the highest cost ads).

Competitor Click Fraud

Competitor click fraud is the selection of links ("clicks") by companies that compete with the link sponsor who have an interest in using the link for malicious or non-intended purposes. These intentions may include depleting the PPC advertising funds or distorting the marketing results of link marketing programs.

Invalid Clicks

Invalid clicks are the selection of links ("clicks") by users or systems (such as automated scripts) for a purpose other than its intended purpose. Invalid clicks may occur if an ad is misleading or uses words or acronyms that are associated with other products or industries.

Hitbots

Hitbots are robots or automated processes that are used to increase the number of page (hit) requests to a web site. Hitbots may be used to increase the perceived value (popularity) of web pages by increasing the number of requested page views.

Impression Fraud

Impression fraud is the process of increasing the number of ad or search result impressions by users or systems who do not have an interest in using the search results for its intended purpose. Impression fraud may be performed by companies or people to increase the popularity of web links or to disable the display of pay per click ads as a result of low click through rates.

Impression fraud inflates the number of impressions without clicks and this reduces the click through rate. Very low click through rates can also result in ads getting dropped from PPC marketing programs.

Click Fraud Type	Description
Accidental	User selects a link by accident. Tends to happen at the highest bid.
Impression Fraud	Companies increase the number of page requests to increase search ranking. May result in disabling keyword due to low CTR.
Competitor Click Fraud	Competitors click web pages to increase marketing costs and to distort marketing performance.
Invalid Clicks	Users clicked because they misunderstood the ad.
Hit Bots	Automated process of clicking ads.
Affiliate Clicks	Affiliates or their employees click on ads to increase performance and ad revenue.
Click Farms	People hired to click ads to make the affiliate search advertiser money.

Figure 1.28, Adword Marketing Click Fraud

Affiliate Click Fraud

Affiliate click fraud is the selection of links ("clicks") by companies that have a co-marketing (affiliate) relationship with the link sponsor who have an interest in selecting the link for non-intended purposes. These intentions may include inflating the value of the affiliate relationship (higher click rates) or getting paid for an increase of the affiliate leads that are provided.

Click Farms

Click farms are groups of people who are hired to click links or ads on web pages.

Figure 1.28 shows some of the ways that adword click fraud may occur. Accidental click fraud occurs when a user selects a different link than they intended to select. Impression fraud occurs when a company sets up programs to request that web pages appear more popular to search engines. Competitor click fraud occurs when companies select competitor's ads to increase the marketing cost. Invalid clicks occur when users select ads they did not understand. Hit bots automatically select ads. Affiliate click fraud occurs when affiliate partners or people they influence select ads to increase their performance and to earn additional advertising revenue. Click farms are groups of people who are paid to click ads to earn revenue from affiliate search marketing networks.

Click Fraud Detection

Click fraud detection is the process of identifying the visitor and storing the information about the visitor to allow comparison of click selections that occur at another time.

Click fraud may be identified by looking for sharp changes in keyword performance. Sudden changes (increases) in keyword performance or click through rates can indicate that click fraud is the cause rather than the viewing or selections by potential customers. Additional indicators of click fraud include changes in navigation patters (stop at landing page) and a decrease in the number of pages viewed.

There are click fraud tools and programs that can be used to identify and analyze the sources of click fraud. Click fraud detection programs or services operate by identifying the visitor and storing the information about the visitor to allow comparison of click selections that occur at another time.

The processes used by click fraud detection programs range from simple IP address logging to storing cookies and gathering identifying computer configuration information from the visitor. They can identify the visitor using IP address, gathering identifying information about the visitor and placing a cookie on the visitor's computer that can be checked during repeated visits.

Adword Marketing Reports

Adword reports can include the number of ad impressions and click through rates for each of the ads.

Adword Impressions

Adword impressions are the number of times a keyword ad is displayed to a viewer. Some adword companies provide an impression share measurement that compares the number of times a media message has been displayed as compared to how many times it could have been displayed.

The number of ad impressions is determined by a variety of factors, which may include the number of people who are searching for information, choice of keywords and bids for keywords. In general, the higher the bid, the larger the number of ad impressions.

Click Through Rate (CTR)

The click through rate (CTR) is the ratio of how many people click on the link or icon to how many are presented. Because adword marketing programs may not charge for ad impressions, the ratio of impressions to clicks mush have a minimum amount or the adword marketing company may drop (disable) some of the keywords.

Conversion Tracking

Conversion tracking is the process of identifying and recording actions of people who visit and navigate through web sites. Conversion tracking usually operates by placing cookies on the visitor's computer when they visit specific web pages and take certain actions (such as receiving an order confirmation page) to discover when, where and how many times the visitor has viewed and interacted with web pages.

Conversion tracking can operate by storing cookie information on the visitors computer and/or by gathering identifying information about the visitor (such as their IP address and web browser version). Conversion tracking enables advertisers to determine the actual effectiveness of their marketing programs.

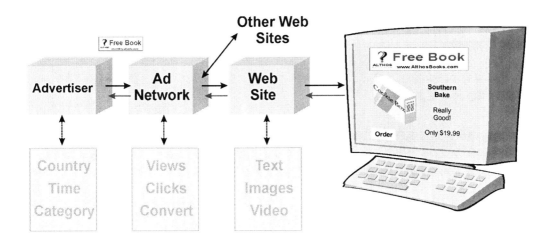

Figure 1.29, Banner Advertising

Banner Advertising

Banner advertising is the process of inserting graphic advertising messages into web pages that are linked to other web pages. A banner ad is a graphic or image that is located on a web site, usually on the top of the page. The banner ad contains a hyperlink that links to another web page or web site and is typically used for advertising products or services. Banner ads can be static (unchanging) or they can be in rich media format (animation or video).

Banner advertising systems link banner ad graphics to web portals or landing pages and use link tracking systems to determine the effectiveness of the banner ads. Banner advertising systems can be self-managed (sold and controlled by the web site operator) or they can be provided using a banner advertising network.

Figure 1.29 shows how a banner advertising system can work. In this example, a company creates and submits a small banner ad to a banner advertising network and selects location, time and category as the ad promotion criteria. The banner advertising network submits these ads to multiple web sites that have agreed to be part of the banner advertising network and keeps track of the transmission, selection and response to these ads. The web site system operators insert the banner ads on their web pages in specific locations.

Banner Ad Types

Banner ad types range from small static images (such as buttons) to interactive animated advertisements. There have been some standard banner sizes that have been defined to simplify the insertion and control of banner ads.

Static Banners

Static banner ads are web advertising images that do not change over time. Static banners may include HTML components (such as text) that can be used to enhance the information experience of the media viewer (better target the banner to the type of viewer).

Animated Banners

Animated banner ads are web advertising images that change over time. Animated banner ads are usually in animated gif format.

Video Banners

A rich media banner is a graphic image that is located on a web site that uses video, graphics and/or audio media to enhance the information experience of the media viewer. Rich media banners may be created using animated GIFs or Flash media.

Banner Sizes

Banner size is the physical dimensions of a banner ad as it appears on the viewers computer display. Banner sizes are quoted in horizontal and vertical pixel size. There are common names associated banner ad sizes of par-

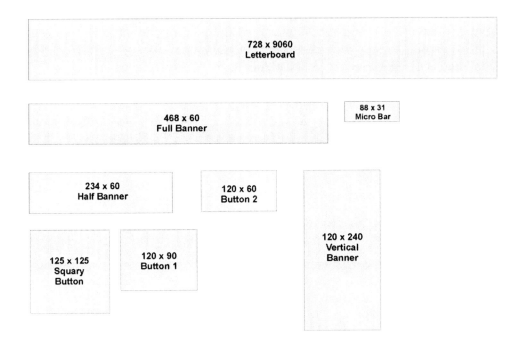

Figure 1.30, Banner Ad Sizes

ticular shapes such as a letterbox (long horizontal banner) and skyscraper (tall vertical banner). Banner ad size standards can be found at the Internet Advertising Bureau (www.IAB.net).

A full banner is a graphic image that is located on a web site that is 468 pixels wide by 60 pixels high. A half banner is a graphic image that is located on a web site that is 234 pixels wide by 60 pixels high. A vertical banner is a graphic image that is located on a web site that is 120 pixels wide by 240 pixels high. A skyscraper ad is a vertical banner graphic image that is located on a web site that is 120 pixels wide by 240 pixels high.

A square banner is a graphic image that is located on a web site that is 125 pixels wide by 125 pixels high. Button size 1 is a graphic image that is selectable on a web site or within another image that is 120 pixels wide by 90 pixels high. Button size 2 is a graphic image that is selectable on a web site or within another image that is 120 pixels wide by 60 pixels high. A micro button is a graphic image that is selectable on a web site or within another image that is 88 pixels wide by 31 pixels high.

Figure 1.30 shows common banner ad sizes. This table shows common IMU sizes for banners and buttons. A full banner is 468 x 60, half banner is 234 x 60 and a micro bar is 88 x 31. Button sizes are 120 x 90 (button 1), 120 x 60 (button 2), and 125 x 125 (square button). A vertical banner is 120 x 240 and a letterboard is 728 x 90.

Banner Exchange Networks

Banner exchange networks are systems that match merchants who want to

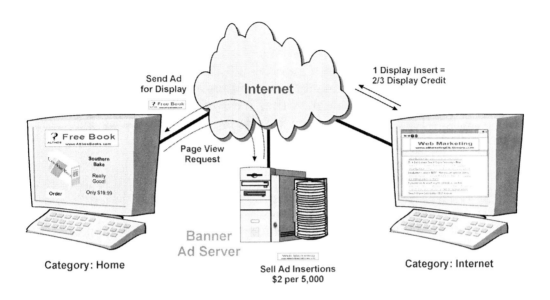

Figure 1.31, Banner Exchange Network

advertise to web site owners who are willing to insert banner ads on their web sites. Banner exchange networks are groups of web site owners who insert and/or pay to insert banner advertising messages on the web sites of other companies. Banner ad networks are commonly managed by hosting companies that coordinate the insertion and tracking of the banner ads.

A banner exchange is the agreement by two (or more) companies to display banner ads on web sites for some form of value. The banner exchange may be a simple agreement for each of the participants to place banner ads that point to each other's company's web site or it may involve additional incentives such as cash, email marketing or the providing of a service.

The banner network exchange operator makes their revenue by charging for the service or keeping (holding back) a percentage of the banner inserts so they can sell them to other companies. For example, for each 100 banner inserts that are placed on one site, the banner exchange network may be allowed to use 33 of them (about $1/3^{rd}$) for their own use (which they may sell to other advertisers).

Figure 1.31 shows how a banner exchange operates. For each banner ad that is displayed, a banner advertiser receives 2/3rds of a credit to place banner ads on other web sites. This example shows that banner ads are categorized so they are displayed on web sites that have related content. The banner exchange network can sell the other 1/3 ad credits to advertising companies to make money.

Banner Ad Categories

Banner ad categories are sets of attributes (such as auto, games, Internet, sports) that are used to define or associate with one or more banner ad campaigns. Banner ad categories may be used in banner exchange networks to direct the insertion of banner ads into web sites that have content that

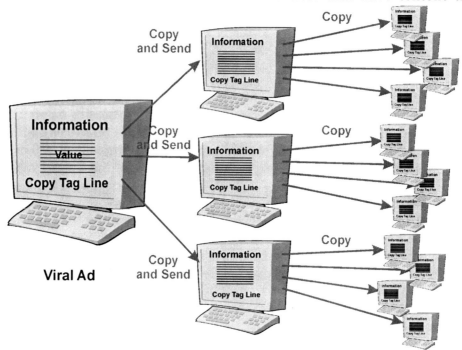

Figure 1.32, Viral (Referral) Marketing

relate to the banner ad (or that relate to what categories the advertiser defines for the banner ad).

Viral Marketing

Viral marketing is the process of producing marketing materials that promote and encourage the retransmission or use of the marketing materials to other recipients.

Viral marketing could be called referral marketing as recipients or viewers of a viral marketing message refer or send the media message on to other people. These recipients will also refer or send the messages to other people resulting in the spreading of a media message. The use of viral messages has the potential for exponential growth in distribution.

Key components of viral marketing include a valuable information element and a referral message (viral message). People who receive a viral marketing message see enough value in the message to forward the message on to other people. An example of viral marketing is the providing of free email addresses in return for allowing a referral message to be included with each message that is sent.

Figure 1.32 shows the basic process of viral (referral) marketing. This diagram shows that viral marketing starts with a message that contains some valuable information element along with a referral message (viral message). The viral message is sent to people who have a likely interest in the information it contains. When people receive a viral marketing message, they are encouraged to forward the message to their friends. This example shows that it is likely that recipients will forward the message on to others who have an interest in the information. This multiplies the effect of the marketing campaign as many more people receive the message than had initially been sent.

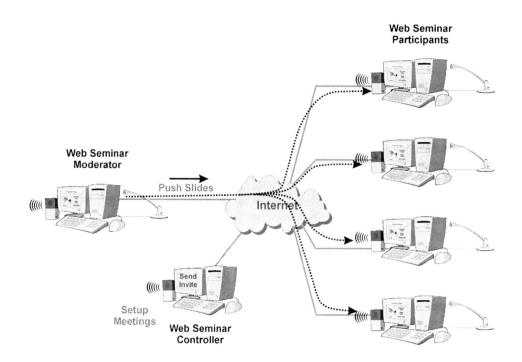

Figure 1.33, Web Seminars ("Webinar")

Web Seminars (Webinar)

A web seminar ("webinar") is an online instruction session that uses the Internet to transfer real time presentation content along with audio channels (via web or telephone) that allow participants to listen. Web seminars may be unidirectional or bi-directional to allow participants to interact with the session.

Web seminars are usually composed of control portals, moderator portals and participant portals. The control portal is a web site area that allows for the setup and management of web seminar sessions. The moderator portal is a web interface that allows speakers or others who are managing the content of a web seminar to send and control content to meeting participants.

The participant portal is a web display that allows people to connect to web seminar host so they can receive content and possibly audio. The audio portion of a web seminar may be provided through the Internet or it may be provided through a telephone system.

Figure 1.33 shows how a web seminar ("webinar") system can allow a moderator or presenter to push content to web seminar participants. The control portal allows for the scheduling and setup of web seminar sessions. As the web seminar moderator progresses through their presentation, the display is pushed to each of the participants of the web seminar.

Mobile Advertising

Mobile advertising is the communication of messages or media content to

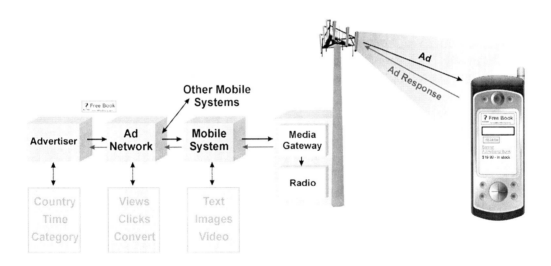

Figure 1.34, Mobile Advertising

one or more potential customers who use mobile devices. Mobile advertising ranges from simple text messaging to intelligent interactive ad messages. The key parts of a mobile advertising system include the advertiser, a mobile ad network, mobile system operators, and mobile devices.

Mobile advertisers create ads and marketing campaigns that define demographic profiles for recipients of the ads (geographic territory, customer types). Mobile ad networks gather the ads and campaign information from the advertisers and send the ads to multiple mobile system operators that have customers that match the marketing campaign profiles. Mobile operators receive the ads along with their marketing requirements, and identify mobile devices that meet the marketing profiles and have the capability to display ads. The mobile devices receive the ads and display them to viewers at appropriate times such as when the user has selected a related information service (e.g. get ring tones).

Figure 1.34 shows how a mobile advertising system can work. In this example, a company creates and submits a small banner ad to a mobile advertising network and selects the location, time and category as the ad promotion criteria. The mobile advertising network submits these ads to multiple mobile networks and keeps track of the transmission, selection and response to these ads. The mobile system operators review the capabilities of the mobile devices in their network to determine which devices can receive and respond to mobile ads.

Podcasting

Podcasting is the recording and making available of media programs (typically audio programs) related to a subject topic on a per download or subscription basis. Podcast marketing is the process of inserting promotional messages into podcast media. Podcast marketers may disguise the promotional content as referring to it as solutions or subjects that are of interest to podcast subscribers.

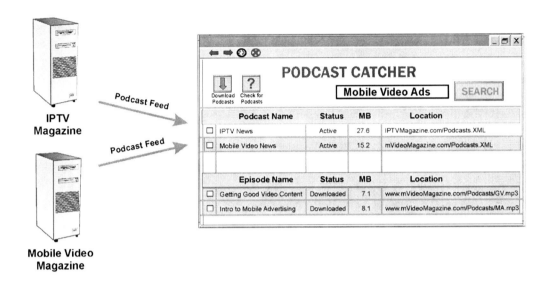

Figure 1.35, POD Casting

Podcast Server

Podcasting involves the creation of media materials (such as audio or video programs), compressing the media, uploading to a podcast server and enabling subscribers to gain access to the materials. A podcast server stores, manages and transmits the media when requested. Podcast servers can be setup on a company web server or podcast services can be provided by using a podcast hosting company. Podcast hosting companies may charge a fee for managing podcasts or they may provide free podcast services in return for advertising messages they may include with the podcast.

Podcatcher

Subscribers setup their computers or media players to subscribe to podcast services using podcatcher software. Podcatcher software monitors podcast channels to discover when a new program is available. The podcatcher software can automatically download into the computer or media device, which allows the podcast subscriber to have immediate access the program (such as a 20 minute audio program). The podcather software may automatically delete the downloaded items from the computer after a period of time.

Figure 1.35 shows how podcasting allows people and companies to create and store content that multiple people can access and transfer. This diagram shows that a podcaster records media, edits and compresses the media, posts the media to a podcast host web site and the media is transferred to people who have subscribed to or requested the podcast program(s).

Discussion Groups

Discussion groups are forums where people can interact and exchange questions, information and suggestions. Discussion groups are typically formed around a theme or industry subject. Web based discussion groups include blogging sites and chat rooms.

Blogging

Blogging is the contributing of information to a subject topic on a shared communication medium such as a text, audio or video log on the internet. Blog marketing is the process of inserting promotional messages into blog postings. Blog marketers may disguise the promotional content by referring to it as solutions or subjects that are of interest to blog visitors.

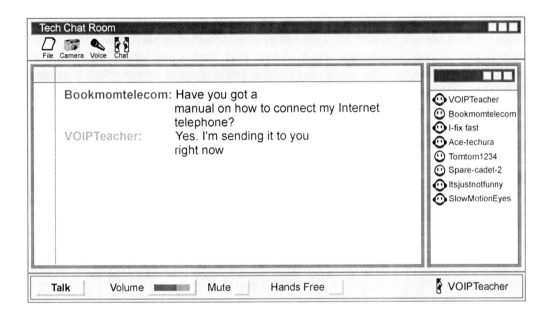

Figure 1.36, Audio Chat Room

Chat Rooms

Chat rooms are real-time communication services that allow several participants (typically 10 to 20) to interact act through the use of text messages or audio. Chat rooms may be public (allow anyone to participate) or private (restricted to those with invitations or access codes.)

Chat rooms allow people who share a common interest to interactively communicate with each other. Chat rooms may use a moderator or they can be independently operated. Chat room servers can be setup on a company web server or chat room services can be provided by using a chat room or community portal hosting company (such as Yahoo). Chat room hosting companies may charge a fee for managing chat rooms or they may provide free chat room services in return for advertising messages they may include on the screen skin or messages they send within the chat sessions.

Figure 1.36 shows how audio chat rooms can operate. In this example, there are several people participating in an Internet telephone chat session. This chat session screen is divided into several smaller windows. The main window is the messaging screen that shows text messages from each participant. The window to the right shows the participants in the chat session. The icon next to each participant (face with or without headset) shows which members have audio and video capability. This screen allows the user to talk by pressing the talk button or by selecting the hands-free option. A display on the bottom is also provided to indicate which participant is talking.

References:

[1]. The Internet Lead Buying Cycle, *Gilbert A. Chavez, October 2005, http://www.dealix.com.*

Appendix 1

Acronyms

Ad Actions-Advertisement Actions
Ad Agency-Advertising Agency
Ad Application-Advertising Application
Ad Campaign-Advertising Campaign
Ad Capabilities-Advertisement
Capabilities
Ad Category-Advertising Categories
Ad Layout-Advertising Layout
Ad Network-Advertising Network
Ad Specs-Advertising Specifications
Ad Structure-Advertisement Structure
Ad Unit-Advertising Unit
Advert-Advertisement
Alt tag-Alternative Text
AMS-Advertising Management System
AO-Application Originated Message
Audioblog-Audio Blog
Auto Bidding-Automatic Bidding
Autoresponder-Auto Responder
Backlink-Back Link
Blog-Web Log
Blog Post-Blog Posting
Blog SPAM-Blog Comment SPAM
Breakeven-Break Event Point
BREW-Binary Runtime Environment for
Wireless
BS1-Button Size 1
BS2-Button Size 2
BSE-Blog Search Engine
CAC-Customer Acquisition Cost
Canonical URL-Canonical Universal
Resource Locator

CAN-SPAM-Controlling the Assault of
Non-Solicited Pornography and Marketing
Act
CBT-Caller Ringback Tone
CFR-Click Fraud Rate
cHTML-Compact Hypertext Markup
Language
Clipart-Clip Art
CMS-Content Management System
CPA-Cost Per Acquisition
CPA-Cost per Action
CPC-Cost Per Click
CPC-Cost per Conversion
CPL-Cost Per Lead
CPM-Cost Per Thousand
CPS-Cost Per Sale
CPTM-Cost Per Targeted Thousand
CPU-Cost Per User
CPV-Cost per Visitor
CR-Conversion Rate
CSC-Common Short Code
CSCA-Common Short Code
Administration
CSS-Cascading Style Sheets
CSSE-Comparison Shopping Search
Engine
CSV-Comma Separated Value
CTA-Call to Action
CTC-Click to Call
CTR-Click Through Rate
CTRC-Click to Receive Coupon
Customer ID-Customer Identification

Daypart-Dayparting
DDC-Default Delivery Context
Destination URL-Destination Universal Resource Locator
DIP-Device Independence Principles
Display Ad-Display Advertisement
Display URL-Display Universal Resource Locator
DIWG-Device Independence Working Group
DOM-Document Object Model
DRAM-Dynamic Random Access Memory
Dynamic Page-Dynamic Web Page
eCash-Electronic Cash
E-Check-Electronic Check
EDGE-Enhanced Data Rates For Global Evolution
EDI-Electronic Data Interchange
EID-Electronic Invoice Data
eLearning-Electronic Learning
Email Opt-in-Email Option In
Email or e-Mail-Electronic Mail
EMS-Enhanced Messaging Service
e-newsletter-Electronic Newsletter
EPC-Earnings per Click
ERM-Email Relationship Management
E-Tailers-Electronic Retailers
ETM-Electronic Ticketing Machine
E-Zine or EZine-Electronic Magazine
Fake URL-Temporary Universal Resource Locator
FMC-Fixed Mobile Convergence
Forwards-Forward Messages
FTEU-Free to End User
Geotargeting-Geographic Targeting
GPS-Global Positioning System
GUI-Graphic User Interface
HDML-Handheld Device Markup Language
Homepage-Home Page
HTML-Hypertext Markup Language

IAB-Interactive Advertising Bureau
iAD-Interactive Advertisements
Image Ads-Image Advertisements
IMAP-Internet Message Access Protocol
Interactive Sites-Interactive Web Sites
InVideo Ad-In Stream Video Advertisements
IO-Insertion Order
IOD-Information On Demand
IP-Intellectual Property
IVR-Interactive Voice Response
IYP-Internet Yellow Pages
J2ME-Java 2 Micro Edition
JCP-Java Community Process
JECF-Java Electronic Commerce Framework
KE-Knowledge Element
Keycode-Key Code
Keyword-Key Word
Keyword URL-Keyword Universal Resource Locator
Killer App-Killer Application
LBA-Location Based Advertising
LBS-Location Based Services
LCP-Lead Capture Page
Listserver-List Server
LPPC-Localized Pay Per Click
LTV-Lifetime Value
M-Advertising-Mobile Advertising
Mailbot-Mail Robot
MASP-Mobile Application Service Provider
M-Card-Mobile Greeting Card
M-Commerce-Mobile Commerce
M-Coupon-Mobile Couponing
Messaging Opt-in-Messaging Option-In
Metatag-Meta Tag
MGW-Mobile Gateway
MIA Email-Missing in Action Emails
Microbutton-Micro Button
MIDP-Mobile Information Device Profile

MIME-Multipurpose Internet Mail Extensions
MMA-Mobile Marketing Association
MMG-Multiplayer Mobile Game
MMS-Multimedia Messaging Service
MNO-Mobile Network Operator
MO-Mobile Originated
Mobile Ad Network-Mobile Advertising Network
Mobile Agency-Mobile Ad Agency
Mobile Search-Mobile Searching
Mobile Site-Mobile Web Site
Mobile TV-Mobile Television
Mobisode-Mobile Episode
Mobizine-Mobile Magazine
Moblog-Mobile Log
MOM-Mobile Originated Message
Monotone-Mono Tone
MT-Application Terminated Message
MT-Mobile Terminated
MTA-Mail Transfer Agent
MTM-Mobile Terminated Message
MWBP-Mobile Web Best Practices
Negative Match-Negative Keyword Match
NRTRDE-Near Real Time Roaming Data Exchange
Opt-in-Option In
Opt-out-Option Out
Opt-out Mechanism-Option Out Mechanism
Pagejacking-Page Jacking
Pagerank-Page Rank
Participation TV-Participation Television
Permalink-Permanent Link
PFI-Pay for Inclusion
PFP-Pay for Performance
PFP-Pay for Placement
PII-Personally Identifiable Information
PO-Purchase Order
POD-Push On Demand
Podcasting-POD Casting

Popdown-Pop-down
Popup-POP-Up
PPA-Pay Per Action
PPC-Pay Per Call
PPC-Pay Per Click
PPD-Pay Per Download
PPI-Pay Per Inclusion
PPV-Pay Per View
Promo-Advertising Promotion
PSMS-Premium Short Messaging Service
PSRAM-Pseudostatic Random Access Memory
PV-Page Views
RAN-Radio Access Network
RAP-Returned Account Procedure
Redirect Server-Redirection Server
ROA-Return on Advertising
ROAS-Return on Advertising Spend
ROI-Return on Investment
RON-Run of Network
RPC-Remote Procedure Call
RSS-Really Simple Syndication
RUIM-Removable User Identity Module
SAC-Subscriber Acquisition Cost
SD-Service Discovery
SEM-Search Engine Marketing
SEO-Search Engine Optimization
SEO Objectives-Search Engine Optimization Objectives
SEP-Search Engine Positioning
SERP-Search Engine Results Page
SessionID-Session Identification Code
SET-Secure Electronic Transaction
Sig File-Signature File
Sitemap-Site Map
SmartPhone-Smart Telephone
SME-Subject Matter Expert
SMIL-Synchronized Multimedia Integration Language
Smishing-SMS Fishing Fraud
SMPP-Short Message Peer to Peer Protocol

SMS-Short Message Service
Softkeys-Soft Keys
SQL-Structured Query Language
SSI-Server Side Include
SSPR-System Selection for Preferred Roaming
Static Page-Static Web Page
STK-SIM Toolkit
Stock Photo-Stock Photography
SYNCH-Synchronization Profile
TAR-Tape Archive Format
Text Ads-Text Advertisements
Text Tagline-Text Tag Line
Tracking URL-Tracking Universal Resource Locator
UGC-User Generated Content
Unique Clicks-Unique Clickthrough
Up-Sell-Up Selling
URL Coupon-Link Coupon
URL Rewrite-Universal Resource Locator Rewriting
User ID-User Identification
USP-Unique Selling Point
VAC-Visitor Acquisition Cost
VAS-Value Added Services
Vidcast-Video Podcast
Video Ads-Video Advertisements
Videoblog-Video Blog
Videocast-Video Casting
Videocasting-Video Casting
Videotone-Video Tone
VisitorID-Visitor Identification Code
vlog-Video Blog
vlogger-Video Blogger
Voice Ad-Voice Advertisements
Wallpaper-Wall Paper
WAP-Wireless Access Protocol
WAP 1.0-Wireless Access Protocol version 1.0
WAP 2.0-Wireless Access Protocol version 2.0
WML-Wireless Markup Language

WSDL-Web Services Description Language
XAML-Transaction Authority Markup Language
xHTML-Extensible Hypertext Markup Language
xHTML MP-XHTML Mobile Profile
XML-Extensible Markup Language

Index

Index

ALTHOS

Althos Publishing Book List

Product ID	Title	# Pages	ISBN	Price	Copyright
Billing					
BK7781338	Billing Dictionary	644	1932813381	$39.99	2006
BK7781339	Creating RFPs for Billing Systems	94	193281339X	$19.99	2007
BK7781373	Introduction to IPTV Billing	60	193281373X	$14.99	2006
BK7781384	Introduction to Telecom Billing, 2nd Edition	68	1932813845	$19.99	2007
BK7781343	Introduction to Utility Billing	92	1932813438	$19.99	2007
BK7769438	Introduction to Wireless Billing	44	097469438X	$14.99	2004
IP Telephony					
BK7781361	Tehrani's IP Telephony Dictionary, 2nd Edition	628	1932813616	$39.99	2005
BK7781311	Creating RFPs for IP Telephony Communication Systems	86	193281311X	$19.99	2004
BK7780530	Internet Telephone Basics	224	0972805303	$29.99	2003
BK7727877	Introduction to IP Telephony, 2nd Edition	112	0974278777	$19.99	2006
BK7780538	Introduction to SIP IP Telephony Systems	144	0972805389	$14.99	2003
BK7769430	Introduction to SS7 and IP	56	0974694304	$12.99	2004
BK7781309	IP Telephony Basics	324	1932813098	$34.99	2004
BK7780532	Voice over Data Networks for Managers	348	097280532X	$49.99	2003
IP Television					
BK7781334	IPTV Dictionary	652	1932813349	$39.99	2006
BK7781362	Creating RFPs for IP Television Systems	86	1932813624	$19.99	2007
BK7781355	Introduction to Data Multicasting	68	1932813551	$19.99	2006
BK7781340	Introduction to Digital Rights Management (DRM)	84	1932813403	$19.99	2006
BK7781351	Introduction to IP Audio	64	1932813519	$19.99	2006
BK7781335	Introduction to IP Television	104	1932813357	$19.99	2006
BK7781341	Introduction to IP Video	88	1932813411	$19.99	2006
BK7781352	Introduction to Mobile Video	68	1932813527	$19.99	2006
BK7781353	Introduction to MPEG	72	1932813535	$19.99	2006
BK7781342	Introduction to Premises Distribution Networks (PDN)	68	193281342X	$19.99	2006
BK7781357	IP Television Directory	154	1932813578	$89.99	2007
BK7781356	IPTV Basics	308	193281356X	$39.99	2007
BK7781389	IPTV Business Opportunities	232	1932813896	$24.99	2007
Legal and Regulatory					
BK7781378	Not so Patently Obvious	224	1932813780	$39.99	2006
BK7780533	Patent or Perish	220	0972805338	$39.95	2003
BK7769433	Practical Patent Strategies Used by Successful Companies	48	0974694339	$14.99	2003
BK7781332	Strategic Patent Planning for Software Companies	58	1932813322	$14.99	2004
Telecom					
BK7781316	Telecom Dictionary	744	1932813160	$39.99	2006
BK7781313	ATM Basics	156	1932813136	$29.99	2004
BK7781345	Introduction to Digital Subscriber Line (DSL)	72	1932813454	$14.99	2005
BK7727872	Introduction to Private Telephone Systems 2nd Edition	86	0974278726	$14.99	2005
BK7727876	Introduction to Public Switched Telephone 2nd Edition	54	0974278769	$14.99	2005
BK7781302	Introduction to SS7	138	1932813020	$19.99	2004
BK7781315	Introduction to Switching Systems	92	1932813152	$19.99	2007
BK7781314	Introduction to Telecom Signaling	88	1932813144	$19.99	2007
BK7727870	Introduction to Transmission Systems	52	097427870X	$14.99	2004
BK7780537	SS7 Basics, 3rd Edition	276	0972805370	$34.99	2003
BK7780535	Telecom Basics, 3rd Edition	354	0972805354	$29.99	2003
BK7780539	Telecom Systems	384	0972805397	$39.99	2006

For a complete list please visit
www.AlthosBooks.com

ALTHOS

Althos Publishing Book List

Product ID	Title	# Pages	ISBN	Price	Copyright
Wireless					
BK7769431	Wireless Dictionary	670	0974694312	$39.99	2005
BK7769434	Introduction to 802.11 Wireless LAN (WLAN)	62	0974694347	$14.99	2004
BK7781374	Introduction to 802.16 WiMax	116	1932813748	$19.99	2006
BK7781307	Introduction to Analog Cellular	84	1932813071	$19.99	2006
BK7769435	Introduction to Bluetooth	60	0974694355	$14.99	2004
BK7781305	Introduction to Code Division Multiple Access (CDMA)	100	1932813055	$14.99	2004
BK7781308	Introduction to EVDO	84	193281308X	$14.99	2004
BK7781306	Introduction to GPRS and EDGE	98	1932813063	$14.99	2004
BK7781370	Introduction to Global Positioning System (GPS)	92	1932813705	$19.99	2007
BK7781304	Introduction to GSM	110	1932813047	$14.99	2004
BK7781391	Introduction to HSPDA	88	1932813918	$19.99	2007
BK7781390	Introduction to IP Multimedia Subsystem (IMS)	116	193281390X	$19.99	2006
BK7769439	Introduction to Mobile Data	62	0974694398	$14.99	2005
BK7769432	Introduction to Mobile Telephone Systems	48	0974694320	$10.99	2003
BK7769437	Introduction to Paging Systems	42	0974694371	$14.99	2004
BK7769436	Introduction to Private Land Mobile Radio	52	0974694363	$14.99	2004
BK7727878	Introduction to Satellite Systems	72	0974278785	$14.99	2005
BK7781312	Introduction to WCDMA	112	1932813128	$14.99	2004
BK7727879	Introduction to Wireless Systems, 2nd Edition	76	0974278793	$19.99	2006
BK7781337	Mobile Systems	468	1932813373	$39.99	2007
BK7780534	Wireless Systems	536	0972805346	$34.99	2004
BK7781303	Wireless Technology Basics	50	1932813039	$12.99	2004
Optical					
BK7781365	Optical Dictionary	712	1932813659	$39.99	2007
BK7781386	Fiber Optic Basics	316	1932813861	$34.99	2006
BK7781329	Introduction to Optical Communication	132	1932813292	$14.99	2006
Marketing					
BK7781323	Web Marketing Dictionary	688	1932813233	$39.99	2007
BK7781318	Introduction to eMail Marketing	88	1932813187	$19.99	2007
BK7781322	Introduction to Internet AdWord Marketing	92	1932813225	$19.99	2007
BK7781320	Introduction to Internet Affiliate Marketing	88	1932813209	$19.99	2007
BK7781317	Introduction to Internet Marketing	104	1932813292	$19.99	2006
BK7781317	Introduction to Search Engine Optimization (SEO)	84	1932813179	$19.99	2007
Programming					
BK7781300	Introduction to xHTML:	58	1932813004	$14.99	2004
BK7727875	Wireless Markup Language (WML)	287	0974278750	$34.99	2003
Datacom					
BK7781331	Datacom Basics	324	1932813314	$39.99	2007
BK7781355	Introduction to Data Multicasting	104	1932813551	$19.99	
BK7727873	Introduction to Data Networks, 2nd Edition	64	0974278734	$19.99	2006
Cable Television					
BK7781371	Cable Television Dictionary	628	1932813713	$39.99	2007
BK7780536	Introduction to Cable Television, 2nd Edition	96	0972805362	$19.99	2006
BK7781380	Introduction to DOCSIS	104	1932813802	$19.99	2007
Business					
BK7781368	Career Coach	92	1932813683	$14.99	2006
BK7781359	How to Get Private Business Loans	56	1932813594	$14.99	2005
BK7781369	Sales Representative Agreements	96	1932813691	$19.99	2007
BK7781364	Efficient Selling	156	1932813640	$24.99	2007

For a complete list please visit
www.AlthosBooks.com

Lightning Source UK Ltd.
Milton Keynes UK
18 September 2009

143883UK00001B/115/P

9 781932 813258